So

SOFTBALL
FOR GIRLS & WOMEN

Gladys C. Meyer

MACMILLAN • USA

Macmillan General Reference
A Simon & Schuster Macmillan Company
1633 Broadway
New York, NY 10019-6785

Library of Congress Cataloging-in-publication Data

Meyer, Gladys (Gladys C.)
  Softball for girls & women.

  Includes index.
  1. Softball for women. I. Title. II. Title: Softball for girls and women.
GV881.3.M49   796.357′8   81-23319
ISBN 0-684-18140-1   AACR2

10

Printed in the United States of America

To the coaches
who shared their softball knowledge
and experience with me as a player

Acknowledgments

I would like to extend my appreciation to the following for their valuable assistance:

Gary Rosenthal, for his advice concerning the initial organization of the book.

Elizabeth Zwingraf, Assistant Professor at the College of Staten Island and Coach of the Linden Majors, for coordinating the photography sessions.

The following Linden Majors, who demonstrated their softball skills:

Marybeth Kaboleski, 1980 MVP, Washington, D.C., Invitational Tournament

Linda Lensch, with six years of playing experience at the major level

Kathy Matthews, 1980 MVP Pitcher, Washington, D.C., Invitational Tournament

Ila Rasmussen, 1981 MVP, Washington, D.C., Invitational Tournament

Karen Youngman, 1981 All-Star DH with Trenton State College

Teri Lynn Allely, twelve years old, who also demonstrated her softball skills.

And Jack Hurley of Bill's World of Sports, for supplying equipment.

Contents

Introduction   *1*
      Development of the Sport   *1*
      Values of Participation   *3*
      Purpose   *6*
1. Throwing, Catching, and Fielding   *7*
      Individual Defensive Skills   *7*
      Fundamentals of Throwing   *7*
      Fundamentals of Catching   *13*
      Throwing and Catching Drills   *17*
      Fundamentals of Fielding   *18*
2. Putting the Defense Together   *27*
      Position Play and General Team Defense   *27*
      Covering the Bases   *30*
      Position Play Drills   *40*
      The Outfield   *45*
      The Force Play   *50*
      The Double Play   *51*
      Backing Up   *54*
      Relay Systems   *57*

The Cut-Off   62
The Rundown   65
Bunt Situations   68
First and Third Situations   72

3. **Batting**   74
Techniques   75
Batting Drills   82
Bunting   83
Bunting Drills   89

4. **Base Running**   91
Running Out a Single   92
Running an Extra-Base Hit   93
Taking a Lead   94
Tagging Up   96
Sliding   96
Base Running Drills   101

5. **The Pitcher**   104
Presentation of the Ball   105
The Basic Grip   106
Pitching Styles   107
Types of Pitches   114
Fundamental Pitching Strategy   116
Speed Versus Control   117
Responsibilities of the Pitcher   118
Pitching Drills   119

6. **The Catcher**   121
Receiving the Ball   122
Setting the Target   125
Throwing   126
Fielding   127
Covering Home Plate   129
Backing Up   130
Calling Signals   131
Responsibilities of the Catcher   132
Catching Drills   133

7. **Putting It All Together**   135
Overall Offensive and Defensive Play   135
Relationship Between Offense and Defense   139

8. **Training and Conditioning** *142*
   General and Specific Conditioning *142*
   Warm-ups *145*
   Stretching Exercises *147*
   Strengthening Exercises *151*
   Exercises Involving Softball Techniques *154*
   Common Softball Injuries and Their
      Prevention *157*
   First-aid Treatment *160*
9. **Equipment** *164*
   Gloves and Mitts *166*
   Bats *170*
   Catcher's Protective Equipment *173*
   Shoes *177*
   Balls *180*
   Uniforms *181*
   Scorebooks *182*
   Miscellaneous Equipment *182*
10. **Organizing to Play** *184*
   Preseason Considerations *184*
   Tryouts *187*
   Practice *190*
   Indoor Practice *191*
   Games *192*
   Leagues *194*
   Other Organizations *195*

Glossary *198*
Rules *201*
Index *205*

Introduction

Softball evolved around the turn of the twentieth century as an adaptation of baseball, and in its early days it was called such names as Kitten Ball, Ladies' Baseball, and Soft Baseball. During the depression of the 1930s, the sport became popular among adults as it afforded a cheap source of recreation. At the 1933 World's Fair in Chicago, the first national tournament was held, and both men's and women's teams competed for their respective championships. But confusion arose because each team played under various rules. To eliminate the problem, the Amateur Softball Association was formed that same year. Two of its early goals were to establish a standardized set of playing rules and to conduct national tournaments. In 1934, one year after the name of the sport officially became "softball," the Amateur Softball Association published the first set of standardized rules.

During World War II, American GIs introduced the sport throughout the world, and after the war the sport

1

flourished both here and abroad. In 1951 the National Softball Week was initiated. The early 1950s saw the organization of the International Federation of Softball. At the first meeting in 1952, the Federation stated three goals: (1) the organization of all of the national associations; (2) recognition by the International Olympic Committee; and (3) the inclusion of softball in the Olympics as well as in all other types of national and international sporting events. The fifties also saw the arrival of slow pitch softball, and the first National Slow Pitch Championship for Women was held in 1957. In the same year a national softball hall of fame was established to honor those men and women who had made outstanding contributions to the growth and development of the sport.

In the 1960s softball grew as an international sport, mainly through the participation of women. In 1965 the Raybestos Breakettes of Stratford, Connecticut, participated in a world tour to further women's softball. That same year, the team participated in the first Women's World Fast Pitch Tournament, in Melbourne, Australia. A year later, demonstration games by top women's teams were part of the Asian Games held in Bangkok and the Pan American Games in Winnipeg.

The 1970s were years of continued international growth for softball. Finally, in 1977, softball was officially recognized by the International Olympic Committee. The Amateur Softball Association sent instructors in coaching and umpiring to Africa, South America, Eastern Europe, and the U.S.S.R. in 1979, and softball competition was included in the Pan American Games for the first time. Back in the United States, the Association of Intercollegiate Athletics for Women, in conjunction with the Amateur Softball Association, sponsored the first College Women's World Series in Omaha.

On an amateur level, softball has truly become a sport for everyone, for children as well as adults, for men as well as women, for the people of the world as well as those of the United States.

VALUES OF PARTICIPATION

For years, women and girls who were interested in sports had to endure the brunt of society's double standard. On the one hand, men and boys were encouraged to compete, while women and girls were encouraged to sit on the sidelines and cheer. Men and boys could enjoy and revel in a sense of accomplishment, while girls and women were generally criticized if they showed too much interest in acquiring sports skills. Public and private institutions and groups sponsored sports activities for boys and men, providing facilities, equipment, and coaches to facilitate learning and participation, but very few coaches or opportunities were available to aid girls and women in the acquisition of sports knowledge.

Slowly, attitudes toward girls and women participating in sports are changing. Studies conducted by sports-oriented physicians, psychologists, and sociologists are demonstrating that both men and women can derive benefits from participation in sports. Myths concerning women athletes, such as the development of bulging muscles or difficulty with childbearing, mental instability, or sexual identity in later life have been debunked. Contrary to some popular beliefs, participation in regular exercise tends to enhance the female body by replacing body fat with firmer muscle tissue and by providing improved muscle tone. Also, the degree to which a woman may increase the strength and bulk of her musculature is dependent upon the percentage of various hormones in her body, a factor which exercise cannot alter. Studies conducted on accomplished athletes tend to indicate that such women have fewer problems during pregnancy and childbirth than many less active women. Other studies tend to demonstrate that participation in competitive experiences increases one's ability to successfully cope with stressful situations. Concerning sexual identity, it has been demonstrated that one's sex role is significantly determined by a combination of hormonal balance before birth and early environmental factors in childhood, well before the age of puberty.

Title IX of the Education Amendments of 1972 prohibits discrimination because of sex in any federally funded programs. Section 86.41, perhaps the most controversial and nebulous part of this amendment, concerns athletics and has served to focus attention on the inequities that have existed in schools and colleges. This attention has raised the consciousness of men and women, in and out of the educational sphere, to the needs and expectations of female athletes. Although there are still legal challenges pending, women athletes have benefited, as illustrated by the increase in the number of sports and scholarships offered, as well as better schedules, accommodations, equipment, and travel arrangements.

Through participation in sports, and specifically in softball, people learn to operate within a set of rules. At times, in softball as in life in general, these rules can place limitations on the individual while providing safeguards for the team or social group as a whole. The individual is also afforded the opportunity to learn to work with others to reach a common goal: to play well. A player who is requested to switch to second base from shortstop may gain more satisfaction from helping her team develop a more cohesive infield than she would from merely playing her favorite position.

The joy of winning is an experience everyone should have at one time or another. Since it takes two teams to play a game of softball, it is obvious that one team will win and the other must lose. Thus, the athlete playing softball learns to react to two situations: how to win and how to lose. At the end of each game it is a common practice for each team to approach the other and congratulate the individuals on having played well. The emphasis is on "having played," not on having won or lost.

Very few, if any, players make it through a season without committing errors, whether physical or mental, but errors provide the athlete with the opportunity to learn to develop the poise and maturity necessary to overcome adversity without falling to pieces. As women continue to gain entrance into fields previously closed to them, this becomes a very important quality both on and off the softball field.

The vast majority of softball players are amateurs and play the game simply because they love it. It affords the student, the clerk, the teacher, the housewife, the lawyer, or the doctor a time to release tension and to get away from the problems of life. For approximately ninety minutes, a player's biggest problems are to catch that ball hit in one's direction, to hit that pitched ball where an opposing fielder can't catch it, to surprise the opponents with a different strategy, or to read an opponent's offense early enough to defend against it.

Conditioning, learning skills, and putting it all together in a game situation can afford a deep appreciation of what the human body can accomplish. Learning to use one's strengths to help minimize one's weaknesses provides additional appreciation of what one can accomplish. The player who cannot hit the long ball learns to contribute by becoming adept at bunting or by just meeting the pitch and hitting those line drive singles too long for the infielder's reach and too short for the outfielder to catch on a fly.

Because softball is relatively well organized, with local, state, national, and international championships, players often have the opportunity to travel. Some travel within a city or one state; others cover several states in league play; still others participate in tours, nationally and internationally; and still others travel to participate in state, regional, or national tournaments. Depending upon the level of play, the sport of softball is able to provide many broadening experiences for its participants.

There are many reasons why people play softball; those mentioned here make up only a partial list. The important factor is that girls and women are participating, and are playing. Some are quiet, some boisterous; some intelligent, tall, short, fair or dark, thin or heavy, but they are all playing. They are not playing like boys or men, but rather like softball players.

PURPOSE

It is hoped that this book will help those who play or coach girls' and women's softball teams by providing a source to consult for the development of softball skills. Many women, as they watch their daughters grow up and develop an interest in softball, want to help their daughters in their endeavors. Unfortunately, many of those concerned and interested mothers did not receive the opportunity to participate and develop skills of their own and their only source of instruction has been by observing men's games and by speaking with some interested male players.

In this book, the game has been broken down into its components, discussing and showing by pictures and diagrams the basic skills and ways to practice such skills. Then the numerous skills are drawn together to provide some insight into how each skill complements the others and leads to team performance. For the neophyte coach, attention has been focused on how to organize practices and games as well as on the development of a league and other sources of current material on softball and sports geared toward girls and women.

It is also hoped that this book will encourage both coaches and players to play well and play hard. At the same time, it is hoped that the book will aid all participants to develop a concern for their own safety and emotional and physical well-being, as well as that of their opponents. Winning is great, but it's not everything. How you play is more important.

1

Throwing, Catching, and Fielding

INDIVIDUAL DEFENSIVE SKILLS

Throwing the ball accurately and catching it are the two major skills necessary for active and successful participation in the game. These two skills pose a sort of "chicken-egg" problem for the softball coach: Which should be taught first? If a player cannot catch the ball, she cannot throw the ball, no matter how strong or accurate her arm may be. If the player cannot throw the ball accurately, the value of her catching or fielding ability will be greatly diminished. But, since these skills complement each other, they can be worked on simultaneously.

FUNDAMENTALS OF THROWING

There are two basic styles of throwing the ball: overhand and sidearm. The overhand motion is generally easier and more accurate for most players. The sidearm motion has the advantage of permitting the player to "get rid" of the ball

7

faster, particularly when she is fielding ground balls, but it is usually more difficult to control. Although the arm motions may differ, the grip on the ball and the footwork are essentially identical.

The Grip

The fingertips are used to grip the ball. The remaining sections of the fingers and the palm hardly make contact with the ball.

To obtain the most secure grip, especially when the ball is new or wet, place the fingertips directly on the seams. The tips of the index and middle fingers are placed on the top seam of the ball while the tip of the thumb is placed on the underside seam. The third and fourth fingers are folded toward the palm. The fourth or little finger does not touch the ball. However, the second section of the third finger rests against the ball, providing further support.

If the player's hand is too small to comfortably accommodate to the two-finger grip, three fingers should be used, with the tips of the first three fingers placed on the top seam

Two-finger grip. *The index and middle fingers are on the top seam; the ring and little fingers are curled to the side; the thumb is underneath.*

Three-finger grip. *The index, middle, and ring fingers are on the top seam; the little finger is curled to the side; the thumb is underneath.*

and the tip of the thumb on the underside seam. The second joint of the little finger, which is folded in toward the palm, rests against the ball for additional support.

Footwork

Both the accuracy and the speed of the throw can be enhanced by proper footwork. Increased distance and ease of throwing are also products of good footwork. Many players consider only the arm when trying to improve their throwing ability, but stepping out correctly enables the entire body to assist in the throw.

Footwork basically involves only one step with the forward or opposite foot. For a right-handed player, that all-important step should be taken with the left foot; the left-handed player uses the right foot. When the arm is cocked, or brought back, just prior to the initiation of the throwing motion, the weight should be on the rear foot. The forward knee should be slightly flexed, and the step with the forward foot should be made in the direction of the intended throw, with the toes pointing toward the target. This step precedes the throw by a fraction of a second.

Arm Motions

The overhand throw begins with the player's head turned toward the intended target of the throw, permitting her eyes to remain fixed upon the target, and her upper body rotated sideways to the target. For balance, the player's gloved hand is extended in the direction of the intended throw. The throwing arm is flexed at the elbow, allowing the elbow to point out and away from the target. The ball is held several inches behind the head, with the wrist cocked (the wrist is extended so that the back of the hand is closer to the outside of the forearm).

As the body weight is transferred onto the forward foot, the upper body is rotated to the left and the throwing arm is extended up and then out toward the intended target. The wrist is snapped forward as the ball is released, the thumb coming off the ball first, then the fingertips. The

Overhand throw position. *The body is turned sideways to the target; the weight is on the right (or rear) foot; the right arm is cocked.*

throwing arm continues outward and downward, across the body. On the follow-through, the rear foot may be brought forward, almost in line with the forward foot.

The sidearm throwing motion enables a player to get the ball away faster because she does not have to straighten up to throw. This throwing motion is most popular among infielders, who, after fielding ground balls, want to get the ball away as quickly as possible. In these situations the distances are not great, since the longest throw would be diagonally across the diamond, approximately 84 feet. If a throw is necessary from deep short, the player would probably revert to the overhand throw for maximum power.

With the player's weight on the rear foot, the upper body is rotated to the right (for a right-handed player) and flexed slightly forward. The throwing arm, with the elbow slightly flexed and higher than the wrist, is brought back between waist and shoulder level. Again, the wrist is cocked

Overhand throw motion. *The body rotates toward the target; the weight transfers onto the left (or forward) foot; the arm reaches upward. The wrist is snapped on the release and the arm continues forward.*

Sidearm throw position. *The weight is on the rear foot and the throwing arm is cocked; eyes are on the intended target.*

Sidearm throw motion #1. *The weight transfers onto the forward foot as the arm comes through to the side.*

Sidearm throw motion #2. *After the wrist is snapped on the release, the arm continues in the direction of the throw.*

and the back of the hand faces up. As the weight is transferred onto the forward foot, the upper body rotates toward the left (for a right-handed thrower), and the arm is brought around to the side, almost parallel to the ground. As the arm passes to the side of the body, the forearm rotates and the wrist snaps or flexes vigorously as the ball is released. The arm follows through in the direction of the intended throw.

FUNDAMENTALS OF CATCHING

In order to catch the softball properly, a right-handed player must use her left hand and a left-handed player must use her right hand. To be able to throw the ball after it has been caught, a right-handed player must have her right hand free. Thus, she wears her glove on her left hand.

When catching a ball, the glove should be kept between the ball and the body, with the back of the glove facing toward the body and the pocket toward the ball. If the ball is above waist level, the fingers of the glove should point upward; if below waist level, the fingers should point downward. The elbows of the arms are partially flexed, placing the glove approximately 15 or so inches from the body. Holding the glove away from the body on initial contact with the ball permits the player to "give." This "giving" action, or pulling of the glove toward the body, helps to absorb the ball's impact and prevent the ball from bouncing out of the glove pocket. If a player catches the ball with her arms stiff, the ball tends to rebound from the surface of the glove, similar to the way it would rebound from a wall or any other hard surface. This "giving" action also initiates the preparation for the throw. Instead of merely permitting the glove to collapse toward the body in any direction, a player should direct the "giving" motion to a specific area. The glove should be guided toward the shoulder of the throwing arm if an overhand throw is intended, or to the side of the body, about waist high, for a sidearm throw.

Catching above waist level.
The fingers of the glove point upward in line with the throwing shoulder; the throwing hand is to the side and behind the glove.

Catching below waist level.
The fingers of the glove point downward; the glove is in front of the space between the legs; the throwing hand is to the side and behind the glove.

When catching a ball, the player should line up with the ball whenever possible. That is, the ball, the glove, and the body of the player should be in a straight line. From the time the player lines up with the ball, the throwing hand should be behind the glove, toward the thumb side. This technique also aids in getting the ball away quickly because, as soon as the ball has hit the pocket of the glove, the throwing hand can slide around the side of the glove and over the ball. This action accomplishes two things. One, the hand closing over the ball in the glove pocket prevents the ball from bouncing out. Two, the hand on the ball permits the throwing hand to start to grip the ball as the glove "gives" toward the point where the throw is to be initiated.

If the ball were caught by the gloved hand on one side of the body and the throwing hand were kept away from the glove, two separate, time-consuming motions would be required to prepare for the throw: the ball in the glove would have to be brought over toward the point where the throw would be initiated, and the throwing arm would have to be brought to meet the gloved ball. In a game where seconds, even split seconds, make the difference between a runner being out or safe, the faster the caught ball begins its journey, the stronger will be the defense.

Although a player should line up with the ball to be caught, sometimes the ball is hit too far to one side to do so. In this instance, as the player's path intersects that of the

Giving action for an overhand throw. *The giving action of the catch guides the glove and the ball toward the throwing shoulder for an overhand throw.*

Giving action for a sidearm throw. *The giving action of the catch guides the glove and ball toward the waist, ready to initiate a sidearm throw.*

Catching on the nonglove side. *The arm is rotated when back-handing or reaching to the nonglove side in order to open the pocket of the glove to the ball.*

ball, she must extend her gloved hand to that side. Since a player can reach further to the side by extending only one arm, there are times when a one-handed attempt is necessary. Naturally, it is preferable for a player to be forced to take several steps after catching a ball in order to gain her balance and prepare for the throw than to be in good position to throw but have no ball to throw.

Another variation in catching the ball is when the ball is hit or thrown to the player's nonglove side. In this situation, the player must extend her gloved hand across her body to backhand the ball. As the player does this, she must also rotate her forearm to open the pocket of the glove to the ball. If the ball to be caught is not too far to the nonglove side, the player can apply the technique of having the throwing hand behind the glove on contact. If the ball is so far to the nonglove side that a maximum or near-maximum reach is required, then the gloved hand by itself is extended toward the ball.

THROWING AND CATCHING DRILLS

When setting up throwing and catching drills, the coach must see that players throw in the same direction and that missed balls will not hit other players or breakable items or cause players to run into streets. When indoors, soft softballs may be preferable.

Drill #1. Beginners may start by throwing at a target, consisting of concentric circles or rectangles, painted on a wall. The player first works to consistently hit within the outer perimeter of the target, then gradually works toward hitting the inner or smallest target. The starting distance can be as close as 10 feet, with the distance increasing as skill develops.

Drill #2. Two players face each other, about 15 feet apart, and throw the ball back and forth between them. As accuracy and skill increase, the distance should be widened. Also, balls may be thrown intentionally to force a player to move to her right or left, or to move backward or forward.

Drill #3. If there are many more players than balls, form two single file lines, with the first player on each line facing each other, about 20 feet apart. The first player in Line A throws the ball to the first player in Line B. Player 1 in Line A then runs to the end of her own line. When Player 1 in Line B catches the ball, she throws it to Player 2 in Line A. After the throw, Line B's Player 1 runs to the end of her own line. The drill continues for all the players in both lines. If space permits, Player 1 in Line A can run to the end of Line B, Player 1 in Line B to the end of Line A, and so on. This additional running also aids in conditioning.

Drill #4. Players in twos or in two lines throw for speed and accuracy. Use a stopwatch to see how many throws and catches can be adeptly executed within a period of 30 seconds or one or two minutes. The players can count out loud every successful throw and catch.

Drill #5. Players in twos or in two lines throw and catch to determine which two players or two lines can keep the ball going back and forth the longest. A dropped ball or wild throw ends this "forever" type of throw and catch drill. This is also a good drill for improving accuracy.

Drill #6. Where large solid wall space is available, such as in gymnasiums or on handball courts, a player throws the ball at a target 15 feet high and attempts to catch the rebound. For variation, Player 1 can throw the ball and Player 2 can catch it on the rebound. The players then reverse roles, with Player 2 throwing and Player 1 catching.

Drill #7. Using four players, one player stands on each base. Player 1 at home plate throws the ball to Player 4 on third base, who catches the ball, adjusts her feet, and throws to Player 3 on second. Player 3 catches the ball, adjusts her feet, and throws to Player 2 on first base. Player 2 catches the ball, adjusts her feet, and throws to Player 1 at home. The direction of the throws can be reversed to help the players adjust to throwing in the opposite direction and to catching balls coming from another direction. If more than four players are participating, several players can line up several feet behind each of the initial players. After a player has completed her catch and throw, she moves either to the rear of her own line or the rear of the line on the base to which she has thrown the ball.

FUNDAMENTALS OF FIELDING

The basic premise of fielding is to first catch the ball and then throw the ball accurately so that it reaches its intended destination as quickly as possible. Fielding can be broken down into two general areas—fielding balls that bounce along the ground, or ground balls, and fielding balls that are hit into the air, or fly balls. The fundamental techniques of throwing and catching apply to both areas of fielding.

Fielding Ground Balls

In this section, the fielding of ground balls will be treated from the perspective of an infielder. The ways in which outfielders play ground balls will be discussed in the section on the outfield in Chapter 2.

The basic body position of an infielder is a semicrouch. The knees and hips are partially flexed, permitting the weight to rest primarily on the balls of the feet. To facilitate movement, the feet should be approximately under the shoulders rather than spread wide apart. The arms should be in front of the body and relaxed. The head should be up to enable the player to keep her eyes focused on the ball from the time it leaves the pitcher's hand until it is hit.

To field a ground ball, the player should run toward the ball to intercept it as soon as possible. The more bounces the ball is permitted to take, the greater the oppor-

Infielder's fielding position.
The feet are apart and the weight is forward; the arms are in front of the body; eyes are on the ball.

tunity for a bad bounce because of pebbles or depressions in the ground. As the player runs toward the ball, she should not carry her gloved hand extended out in front because it will cause her to slow down. Instead, the player should use both arms in a regular running, pumping motion. When she has lined up her body with the ball, the player should come to a momentary stop and catch the ball as it comes off a bounce. By stopping with her feet apart, she prevents the ball from being knocked out of her gloved hand by contact with a knee as she "gives" to absorb the impact of the ball. As soon as the ball enters the glove pocket, the throwing hand slides around the side of the glove and on top of the ball. Both hands move toward the starting point for the throw, and the throwing hand starts gripping the ball. When the starting point of the throw is reached, the throwing hand continues moving back, taking with it the ball it has already gripped. At the same time that the ball is being brought back toward the start of the throw, the weight on the feet should be shifted so that by the time the throwing arm is cocked the weight is on the rear foot and the fielder is prepared to step and throw.

If the ground ball is hit only slightly to the side of the fielder, a few short sliding steps may afford the quickest method of adjusting to intersect its path. On the other hand, if the ball is hit considerably to the side of the fielder, she should cross over on her first step and turn her side to the ball, which permits her to run toward the anticipated point of interception. Again, it is important that the arms be used in the normal pumping action as the player runs toward the ball.

Throughout the play, from the time the ball leaves the thrower's hand until it has entered the pocket of her glove, the fielder should keep her eyes focused on the ball. That last bounce before the ball enters the glove is the most important one to watch. If the ball should take a bad bounce, the fielder can still adjust because she is in a position to see the ball move. Often, beginning fielders have a tendency to turn their heads away from the ball at the last minute because they are fearful of being hit by it. Actually, by turning their faces away and thus taking their eyes off the ball, they are more prone to be hit if the ball suddenly changes course.

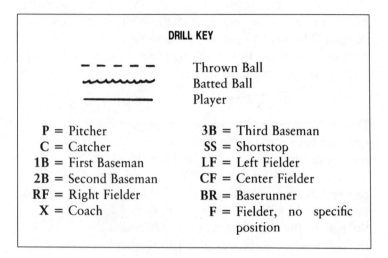

DRILL KEY

— — — — —   Thrown Ball
〜〜〜〜〜   Batted Ball
————————   Player

P = Pitcher	**3B** = Third Baseman
C = Catcher	**SS** = Shortstop
1B = First Baseman	**LF** = Left Fielder
2B = Second Baseman	**CF** = Center Fielder
RF = Right Fielder	**BR** = Baserunner
X = Coach	**F** = Fielder, no specific position

Ground Ball Drills (See also Drill Key)

Drill #1. In twos, one player throws hard bouncing ground balls to the second player. The second player runs in or to the side to field the ball and throws it back to the first player.

Drill #2. Pepper Drill 1. One player, in a bunting stance, faces three to five fielders, each about 10 feet away from her. One of the fielders lobs a soft underhand toss to the bunter. The bunter intercepts the ball with the bat and lets the ball rebound from the bat. The bat should be motionless on contact with the ball. The player sets the angle of the bat before the contact. As the ball is bunted in their direction, players field it and toss it back to the bunter. As player bat control and fielding skills increase, a short push into the ball may be permitted.

Drill #3. Pepper Drill 2. When players have good bat control and fielding skills, the distance between the batter and the fielders can be increased to approximately 25 to 30 feet. The fielders may use overhand or sidearm motions to throw the ball easily but accurately toward the batter. The batter now takes a half swing at the ball, stopping the bat upon contact. This drill affords the fielders a more gamelike practice, since they can follow the ball to the bat and off the bat with their eyes and react accordingly.

Drill #4. To simulate game distances, the distance between the coach (X), who is batting ground balls, and the fielders (F) is approximately 50 to 60 feet. The coach hits the ball and F_1 runs in or to the side, fields the ball, and throws it at the catcher (C). F_1 then goes to the rear of the line. The catcher then tosses the ball to the coach, who hits to the next fielder. (See diagram.)

Drill #5. As in Drill #4, the coach (X) bats ground balls to a line of fielders. This time, the fielder (F), after fielding the ball, throws the ball to the first baseman (1B). The first baseman throws the ball to the catcher (C), who lobs the ball to the coach. After the fielder completes the play, she goes to the rear of the line.

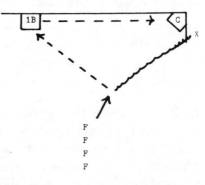

To encourage accurate throws, all wild throws that the first baseman cannot handle are chased by the player who made the poor throw. (See diagram.)

Drill #6. The coach (X) bats ground balls to a line of fielders approximately 60 feet away. The first fielder (F_1) runs in, fields the hard grounder, and throws the ball to the first baseman (1B). The first baseman throws the ball to the

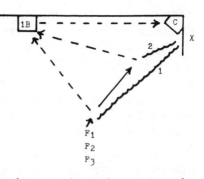

catcher (C). While ball number one is on its way to the catcher, the coach either bunts or hits softly a second ball. F_1 continues in after her first throw, fields the second ball, and again throws to the first baseman before going to the rear of the fielding line. (See diagram.)

In small gymnasiums, where batting would be dangerous, Drills 2–6 can be adapted by having the coach roll or throw the ball and requiring fielders to attempt to field the ball before it crosses a specific floor marking. Speeds of the ball can be varied, depending on the skill level.

Fielding Fly Balls

Although fly balls are fielded by both infielders and outfielders, and most techniques apply equally to both, this section will be primarily from the perspective of the outfielder.

Like the infielder, an outfielder must also assume a good ready position before the ball is hit. The feet should be a comfortable distance apart, about shoulder width. Knees and hips are partially flexed and the arms are out in front with the hands about knee high, but not resting on the knees. The head should be up so that the eyes can be focused on the action. The player's weight should be on the balls of the feet.

The faster an outfielder reacts to the batted ball and begins to move to intercept it, the better position she will be in to make the catch. Through experience in fielding batted fly balls, a player will learn to judge the flight of the ball. The angle at which the ball leaves the bat is also the angle at which it will come down. If a ball leaves the bat at approximately a 45-degree angle, it will return at approximately a 45-degree angle. A ball that leaves the bat at an 80-degree angle will return at an 80-degree angle. The larger the angle of ascent of the batted ball, the closer to the home plate area it will descend; conversely, the smaller the angle of ascent, to approximately 45 degrees, the farther the ball will tend to travel before coming down.

Another important aspect that assists the outfielder in judging the flight of the ball is the sound of the ball when it makes contact with the bat. That solid crisp sound the ball makes when it contacts the heart of the barrel of the bat puts a lump in the pitcher's throat that also tells the outfielder that she is going to have to hustle in order to have a chance at catching this one. The angle of the ball and the sound of the hit are two factors that, when combined, will enable the outfielder to get a jump on the ball.

When the ball is hit a considerable distance from the outfielder, she must run as hard as possible to reach it. To run efficiently, she must use both arms in a pumping action. Only after she has reached the anticipated point of interception of the path of the ball does she extend her gloved hand outward to receive the ball. Also, when the outfielder is running, she should run on her "toes" rather than on her heels. To a player running on her heels, the fly ball will appear to bounce in the air because of the jarring of her body caused by her heels hitting the ground. By utilizing the balls of the feet or "toes," this bouncing effect will be eliminated, enabling the outfielder to judge the flight of the ball more accurately and easily. On a long fly ball that goes over the outfielder's head, she should turn her back on the infield and run in the direction of the anticipated interception point of the ball. Using a regular running technique and watching the ball over her shoulder will enable the outfielder to reach a better position in which to catch the ball. If the ball is hit deep and to the side, a diagonal running pattern is best. Again, use a regular run with arms pumping and head turned to keep the eyes focused on the ball.

The weather is another important factor that must be considered in catching fly balls. On a sunny day, holding the gloved hand high above the upturned face can shade the eyes to permit an outfielder a better view of the ball. Also, fly balls are greatly affected by wind velocity and direction. Strong winds blowing from behind home plate may cause the ball to carry farther, while the same winds blowing toward the home plate area may bring a well-hit ball to a stop. Flags and tree branches blowing in the wind are helpful guides when trying to catch fly balls.

When the outfielder finally reaches the anticipated point of interception with the path of the ball, she should extend the glove toward the ball. The ball should enter the pocket when the glove is in line with the throwing shoulder and slightly higher, but in front of, the head. Again, the throwing hand should be behind the glove on contact with the ball. As contact with the ball is made, the "giving" action should carry the ball toward the throwing shoulder to help the outfielder get the ball away quickly.

Fly Ball Drills (See also Drill Key on page 21)

Drill #1. The coach (X), standing about 100 feet from a line of players, fungo hits fly balls on an angle. One fielder at a time runs to intercept and catch the ball. After the catch, the fielder regains her balance, turns, and throws the ball on one bounce to the catcher (C). After the throw to the

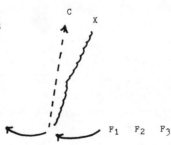

catcher, the player remains on that side of the outfield. When each player has completed her turn, the drill is repeated with the players running in the opposite direction to catch the batted fly balls. (See diagram.)

Drill #2. Set up as in Drill #1. This time, however, fly balls are hit that cause the players to either run in or run out to make the catch.

Drill #3. Drills #1 and #2 can be adapted to a gymnasium. Using a basketball court as a guide, players line up on the long side of the court. Fielder 1 (F_1) starts to run down the side and around the corner of the court, and the coach (X) hits a soft fly ball on the diagonal. F_1 catches the fly ball and throws it to the catcher (C). The fielder then jogs around the court and back to the end of the line. If

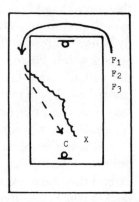

the gymnasium is too small for a ball to be hit, a similar effect can be obtained by tossing the ball instead of hitting it. (See diagram.)

2

Putting the Defense Together

POSITION PLAY AND GENERAL TEAM DEFENSE

Position play is an important concept in the development of a strong team defense. Each player must be aware of her specific responsibilities and contribute to the overall defense by carrying out those responsibilities.

In the infield, a baseman is responsible for considerably more than merely standing with one foot touching her base and catching a ball. She must be aware of the territory she is responsible for covering. By knowing which batted balls she should try for, and which batted balls are better left for another player to attempt to field, an individual player becomes part of a team. A first baseman must know when a particular batted ball will be easier for the second baseman to play, because she can then cover her base and be ready to receive the throw from the second baseman. If players insist on trying for every batted ball, many a batter-baserunner will be safe merely because no defensive player was at the base to receive the throw. A balance must be established between the individual who would like only to stand on her base and catch thrown balls and the individual who tries for every batted ball.

The diagram on page 29 illustrates the fundamental starting positions for each of the nine players and the general area for which they are responsible. It must be kept in mind, however, that this is a guide and not an indisputable set of boundary lines. The speed and skill levels of the individual players are important considerations in slicing up the softball-field pie. Other vital considerations, particularly in the infield, are the players' glove hands and the directions in which they must move. For example, on a batted ball hit up the middle (directly over second base), the shortstop moves to her glove side to reach the ball, with her momentum carrying her in the general direction of first base. If the second baseman goes for the ball, she must move toward her nonglove side to reach the ball, forcing her to backhand the ball. Also, after having caught the ball, the second baseman must stop her forward momentum and prepare to throw in the opposite direction from which her body has been moving in order to reach first base.

Since it is easier, particularly on infield pop-ups, for a player to catch the ball when she is moving forward to intercept the path of the ball, the first and third basemen are responsible for fielding plays quite close to the home plate area. In the same context, it can be seen that the first, second, and third basemen and the shortstop combine to catch most of the pop-ups around and behind the pitcher's plate area. Knowledge of the opposing team will affect the positioning of the players on the field. A batter known to hit down the third base line will cause a shift of the fielders toward that area of the field.

In most instances, the fielders will assume defensive positions as illustrated in the diagram. Both the first and third basemen take starting defensive positions approximately 5 or 6 feet in from the foul line and 2 or 3 feet closer to home plate than their respective bases. The second baseman is positioned on the right side of the infield, perhaps one-third of the way toward first base and several feet

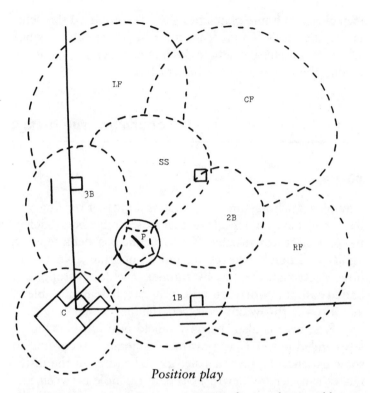

Position play

behind an imaginary line connecting first and second bases. The shortstop plays on the left side of the field, 5 or 6 feet behind an imaginary line between second and third bases and approximately one-third of the way toward third base. The center fielder is generally in line with home plate and second base, positioning herself just far enough to either side of the line to permit an unobstructed view of the pitch and the batter. Depending upon the level of play, she may be anywhere from 20 or 30 feet to 100 feet behind second base. Both the right and left fielders may begin by taking positions roughly 25 to 30 feet in from their respective foul lines, with the depth from home plate depending upon the hitting ability of the opposing batters. The starting positions of the battery—that is, the pitcher and catcher—are specific. The pitcher must begin with her feet in contact with the pitcher's plate, and she is approximately one large step closer to home plate after she has completed the delivery of the pitch. The catcher must be in the catcher's box when the pitcher is ready to pitch and, generally, she is just behind the rear line of the batters' boxes.

COVERING THE BASES

First Base

Any player who assumes the responsibility of playing first base must have a good glove; that is, she must be proficient in catching thrown balls. While height is a definite asset, agility and quick reflexes are more important. No matter how spectacular the play by another infielder in stopping a batted ball, it is worthless unless the first baseman is able to adjust to the throw and complete the play.

First base is also the only infield position in which a left-handed player is at a distinct advantage. According to some experts, the fact that her glove hand is on the inside makes it easier for her to help plug the hole between first and second bases and also makes her a better target for the catcher or other infielders to throw at because the glove is naturally away from the runner.

A first baseman, whether right- or left-handed, must be ready to run toward home plate to field bunts and pop-ups. It is important that she learn to run hard into foul ground, to the right of the foul line, to field the many pop-ups hit into that area. Of course, she must also possess those skills needed for fielding ground balls.

As soon as the ball has been hit by the batter, the first baseman must decide where the ball is going and position herself accordingly. If the anticipated throw will be coming from the vicinity of third base or short, she should position herself in front of the inside front corner or the corner of first base closest to third. For a throw from second, the inside rear corner may be the corner closest to the originating point of the throw. The inside rear corner may also be the best corner of first base from which to receive throws from right field. These corners permit the first baseman to be in the closest position to the play and also keep her foot farthest from the part of the base which the baserunner will touch.

Once the best corner of the bag is decided, the first baseman must assume a ready position. Generally, the body is facing the direction from which the throw will be made, both feet are apart, knees and hips are relaxed, and the glove, open to the throw, is held about shoulder height, slightly in front of the body. The weight should be on the balls of the feet in order to quickly adjust the feet to the throw. While waiting for the throw, the first baseman may stand with her heels touching the side of the base, so that

First base ready position. *Player is facing the direction of the throw; her heels are close to the base; her glove is held up as a target for the throw.*

Stepping out toward the throw. *The player steps with the gloveside foot in the direction of the throw; the arms reach out toward the ball.*

a short backward movement of the foot will ensure contact with the base on the play.

If the throw is good (that is, if it is coming directly at her about face or shoulder height), a right-handed first baseman should place the toes of the right foot on the closest corner of the base. Then, she steps out with her left foot in the direction of the throw, while extending her hands forward to receive the ball. Again, the glove should be open to the throw, with the throwing hand behind the glove ready to slide around the side and over the ball as the arms "give" or pull in to absorb the impact of the throw. As soon as the ball has been caught, the first baseman should remove her foot from the bag to prevent any contact with the runner.

Should the throw be wide, toward the inside or home plate side of first base, the first baseman uses basically the same footwork, except that in this situation, the step with the left foot is as large as possible. If the throw is wide toward the outfield side of the base, a right-handed first baseman uses the toes of the left foot to contact the base, while the wide step toward the ball is made with the right leg. The stretch in this instance is not as great as that obtained with the feet in the reverse position, but the advantage is in the body position in relation to the throw. By stepping out with the right foot, the body remains open to the throw, whereas stepping with the left foot causes the player to turn her back toward the throw and the infield. Of course, if the throw is so wide that a maximum stretch may not be sufficient, the first baseman should not hesitate to leave the base to catch the thrown ball. By leaving the base, she will have a better chance to catch the poor throw. Although the batter-baserunner may be safe at first, she will not be able to continue on to second, a definite possibility if a throw goes past the first baseman. With a runner on first base there is the possibility of a double play on the next batted ball, but with a runner on second, the next batted ball may result in a run for the opposition.

Should the ball be hit so that the first baseman must

handle it, she must communicate with her pitcher and second baseman concerning the coverage of the base. If the first baseman fields the ball close enough to her base, she can complete the play herself. If she is pulled too far to her right, she must flip the ball to the second baseman or pitcher, depending upon who is covering the base. The word *flip* is important here because usually the player covering the base is running toward the base and the distance is short. *Flip* refers to a ball tossed with an underhand motion. This flip throw should lead the player coming toward the base and, for ease of handling, should be about shoulder height as it reaches the base.

Although the majority of plays at first base are force plays, there are instances when a first baseman must tag a runner in order to record the out. If a batter-baserunner rounds first, heads toward second, and decides to return to first, or if a baserunner on first takes a lead with the pitch and must return, the first baseman must be prepared for a possible tag play. With a runner coming back to first, the first baseman should straddle the bag with her feet, thus leaving room for the baserunner to slide onto the base without the danger of contact. The first baseman's upper body must be turned in the direction of the throw so that her eyes can be focused on the throw and to give the thrower a glove target. Knees and hips should be slightly flexed. When the thrown ball has been caught, the glove is swung down to a position between the base and the runner sliding in. In this way, the baserunner actually tags herself out by sliding into the glove containing the ball. On the tag play, the first baseman must make sure that the glove is wrapped around the ball so that the ball cannot be dislodged by contact with the baserunner. It is important to remember that the baserunner does not have to be tagged out by the ball itself, but only by the glove containing the ball. Thus, if the glove is turned so that the finger side is in contact with the side of the base and the thumb side is toward the runner, the runner's foot will touch the back of the thumb side of the glove and not be able to dislodge the ball. On a tag play, the first baseman should also be careful not to place her throwing hand between the glove and the runner.

Second Base

Both the shortstop and the second baseman cover second base, depending on the situation. These two players perhaps work more closely together than any other members of the team. Each must be aware of her own responsibilities— when she must cover the base, back up the throw, and go out for a relay.

Although there are various types of double plays, the most common ones involve either the shortstop or second baseman covering second. If a ground ball is hit on the right side of the field, the second baseman either fields it or backs up the pitcher or first baseman while the shortstop covers second base to take the throw. If a ground ball is hit to the left side, the shortstop either fields it or backs up the third baseman or pitcher while the second baseman covers second.

In covering second base on a double play, the fielder should catch the toss while moving toward the base in order to have control of the ball as she tags the base with her foot. The foot may either step on the top of the base or may just brush across the top and then step on the ground past the base. In either instance, the inside foot should be used to tag the base. For the shortstop, this is her right foot, and for the second baseman, her left. By tagging the base in this manner, the fielder's body is mostly behind the base, farthest from the approaching runner.

After tagging the base with the appropriate foot, the fielder continues moving past the base, out of the path of the baserunner, and prepares to throw to first. The second baseman will make the throw from the third base side of second, while the shortstop will make the throw from the first base side of second.

Both the shortstop and second baseman cover second

Covering second base on a double play. *The shortstop tags the base with her right foot and steps toward first with her left, ready to complete the throw.*

on throws from the outfield. If the ball is hit to right field or right center, the second baseman will probably go out to assist in the formation of a throw relay, while the shortstop covers the base. On balls hit to left, left center, and center field, the second baseman and shortstop reverse duties.

If the throw is coming from left field and there is a possibility of a tag play at second, the second baseman must assume a ready position to catch the throw, but avoid blocking the base in case the play does not materialize. Therefore, she should stand with both feet behind or on the right field side of the base, with her upper body turned toward the direction from which the throw will come. If the throw is on target, she will catch the throw and turn toward first by stepping across the base with her right foot. The glove, containing the ball, is swung down and placed between the runner and the base. The second baseman now has one foot on either side of the base, affording the runner room to slide into the base without personal contact.

On a throw from center field, the fielder will stand

with her feet on the third base side of second, her body facing toward the throw. After the ball has been caught, she will step across the base with her left foot. Again, all techniques necessary for a safe tag play are implemented.

To cover second while expecting a throw from right field, the fielder should have one foot on each side of the base, leaving the base itself free for the sliding runner. Although the toes are facing toward first base, her upper body is again rotated toward the direction of the throw.

These foot and body positions are also appropriate for use when throws are coming from other infielders. On a throw from the first baseman, the player covering second would do exactly that described for a play at second with the throw originating in right field. The same association can be made between a throw from left field and third base.

In instances where the play at second does not require a tag, such as a force out to end an inning, the fielder cov-

Ready position for a throw to second. *The shortstop must reach for the throw from center field.*

Ready position after the ball is caught. *After the catch, the shortstop steps across the base with her left foot; the player crouches and places the glove down in front of the base for the runner to slide into the tag.*

ering second employs the same techniques as those used by the first baseman. She should place the toes of her right foot against the corner of the base closest to the area from which the throw will come, while holding her glove up as a target for the throw. Then, when the line of the throw has been established, she should step forward, in the direction of the throw, with her left foot. As soon as the play has been completed, she should move quickly out of the base-path area.

There are also times when tag plays must be made on upright running baserunners rather than on sliding baserunners. In this situation, if time allows, the fielder should move in front of her base, to the inside of the base path. In this position, the possibility of full body contact on the tag play is greatly diminished, if not completely avoided. From this position, the baseman merely touches the baserunner on the side of the hip area with the back of the glove as the runner runs by. To prevent the ball from being juggled or knocked loose upon contact, the baseman may use her throwing hand to hold the ball in the glove. Although the

Tag play on an upright baserunner. *The shortstop, in front of and to the inside of the base, tags the runner in the side as she tries to run past.*

tag may be firm, a tendency to swing the glove into the runner should be avoided because it can be dangerous to the baseman and is not good sportsmanship.

Third Base

The third baseman must have quick reflexes, be very agile, and possess a good glove (fielding ability) and a strong accurate throwing arm. She must be aggressive because she is in the best position to field the majority of pop-ups in the third base line area, since she can move toward the ball faster than either the pitcher or catcher. She must be ready to charge in to field a bunt, as well as to react to hard ground balls or line drives, which are frequently hit down the third base line. Above all, she is responsible for covering almost all plays at third base.

The type of softball played affects the third baseman's

starting position. If she is playing in a fast pitch blacktop league or in a slow pitch league, she can play several feet behind the base and a few feet in from the foul line because she does not have to be concerned about bunted balls since bunting is not permitted. In regular fast pitch softball on a dirt field, she must be ready to react in bunt situations; thus, her ready position cannot be as deep but should be a step or two inside her base.

Because of the closeness to the home plate area and the fact that the vast majority of batters are right-handed, the third baseman has to field many hard ground balls and line drives. In most situations, standard fielding procedures apply. However, some balls are hit so hard that all the third baseman can do is to knock them down. If she is able to keep the ball in front of her body, she will still have a play. Due to the speed at which the ball reaches her, the third baseman often has time to pick up a knocked-down ball and complete the play to record the out at first base. Even if she is not able to complete the throw to first base, chances are that although the batter-baserunner is safe at first, she has been prevented from continuing on to second. In these situations the third baseman must keep a cool head, either to make a hard accurate throw or to hold up and not complete the throw if she is unable to gain complete possession of the ball or if the runner has reached the base.

Covering third on throws from the outfield or infield employs the same sort of techniques described in the preceding section on second base. The third baseman should straddle the base, one foot on the inside and one foot on the outside of the base. Her upper body should be rotated to face the direction of the throw. After she has caught the ball, she swings her gloved hand down toward the base to place the glove and the ball in front of the base. Again, knees and hips should be slightly flexed with the head up enough to permit the third baseman to follow the sliding runner with her eyes as she slides into the tag.

If the tag play is on an erect baserunner, the third baseman should move out of the base path, to the inside of her base, a step or two toward second. As the runner goes by the third baseman, she should tag her in the hip area by touching her with the back of the glove.

POSITION PLAY DRILLS (See also Drill Key on page 21)

Drill #1. The coach (X) hits ground balls for the first baseman to field. The first baseman fields the ground balls, runs to her base, and completes the play by tagging her base. After the tag, the first baseman throws the ball back to the catcher. The speed of the batted balls should vary with the skill level of the fielder. (See diagram.)

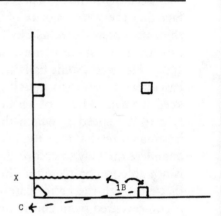

Drill #2. The coach (X) hits ground balls to the right side. Some balls are hit for the first baseman to field, and then tossed to the second baseman covering first. The second baseman, after completing the play at first, throws the ball to the catcher. Occasionally, balls should be hit to permit the first baseman to complete the play by herself. (See diagram.)

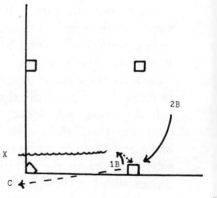

Drill #3. The coach hits ground balls to each infielder (2B, 3B, SS) and the pitcher (P). Each player runs in, fields the ball, and then throws to the first baseman for a force play. The first baseman throws to the catcher. If more players are to be included, players can line up several feet behind each position and take turns. After

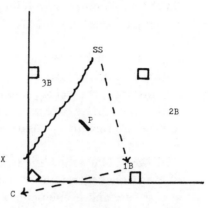

completing the fielding and throwing part of the drill, each player may move to the rear of her line or may rotate to the rear of the next line. (See diagram.)

Drill #4. The coach (X) alternates hitting ground balls to the third baseman and shortstop. Each fields the ball and throws to the second baseman covering second. The second baseman catches the throw or toss, tags second with her left foot, continues out of the base path, and throws to first base. The first baseman throws the ball to the catcher and returns to her

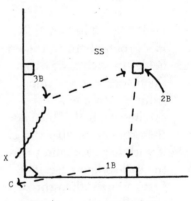

fielding position. (See diagram.) In a variation of this drill, the coach hits ground balls to the right side of the field, with the shortstop now covering second base. Either the first or second baseman fields the ball and throws to second base. The shortstop catches the throw, tags second base with her right foot, and completes the play by throwing to first base. The first baseman throws the ball back to the catcher. Before each ball is batted, the coach should call out the play to remind the players of what is expected. Players should be encouraged to tell each other who will cover the base under what conditions.

Drill #5. Drills #3 and #4 can be varied by the coach hitting line drives instead of ground balls to the fielders. In this instance, the fielder catches the line drive and throws to the appropriate base (called by the coach prior to the hit) to catch an imaginary runner off the base.

Drill #6. Once the basic fielding, throwing, and covering of the bases become more routine, runners may be placed at first base and home plate. As the coach hits the ball, the baserunners leave their bases and the fielders must complete the plays as in Drills #3 and #4 but with actual baserunners to beat to the base with the throws. This drill also assists fielders in learning to avoid any contact with baserunners and to complete the play despite the baserunners.

Drill #7. The coach (X) hits ground balls to the fielder in such a way that the fielder is a few steps from her base when she catches the ball. The fielder then runs to her base, tags it with her foot, and throws the ball to first base. The first baseman then throws the ball to the catcher. (See diagram.)

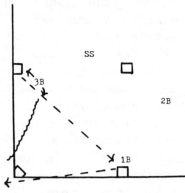

Drill #8. The coach (X) calls the play at first base and hits bunts. The first and third basemen and the catcher field the bunts and throw to the second baseman, who is covering first base. The shortstop covers second, although no play is made there. The second baseman, after tagging first base,

throws the ball home. (See
diagram.) For a variation,
the coach calls the play at
second base. This time, the
shortstop covers second to
take the throw at second
since the second baseman is
covering first base. The
shortstop throws the ball to
the catcher after tagging
second base.

Drill #9. The catcher
throws ground balls to the
fielders, and calls the play
(for example, first). If a
ground ball is thrown to
the third baseman, she
fields the ball and throws to
first base. She then runs
back to her base to cover
third. The first baseman
catches the ball at first and
then throws the ball to the

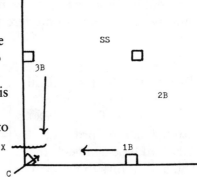

catcher, who in turn throws the ball back to the third baseman covering third. The third baseman then returns the ball
to the catcher. (See diagram.)

If the ball is hit to the shortstop, she fields the ball,
throws to first base, and then covers second base to await
the throw from the catcher. The second baseman may practice backing up the shortstop on the throw from the
catcher. When the ball is hit to the second baseman, the
shortstop/second baseman roles are reversed.

If the ball is hit to the first baseman, she fields the ball
and throws to the second baseman covering first. As soon
as she has tossed the ball, the first baseman begins to run

back to her base in order to take the return throw from the catcher. In returning to cover her base, the first baseman must be careful not to interfere with the second baseman's throw home.

Drill #10. In this drill, all plays are made to first base. The coach (X) first hits a ground ball to third, and the third baseman fields the ball and throws to first. On the hit, the shortstop backs up the third baseman, and the other infielders cover their own bases. (See diagram.)

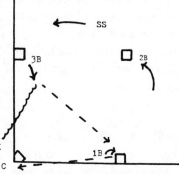

The coach then hits to short. The shortstop fields the ball and throws to first. On the hit, all other fielders run to cover their own bases.

The coach next hits to first. The first baseman fields the ball and calls to complete the play herself or tosses to the second baseman covering first. On the hit, the third baseman covers third, and the shortstop covers second.

Drill #11. With a runner (BR) on second base, the coach hits a ground ball and the baserunner leaves second and heads for third. The fielder must field the ball and throw to the third baseman, who makes a tag play on the runner. The runner can be instructed to slide or to remain standing, thus affording the third baseman the practice in both types of tag plays. (See diagram.)

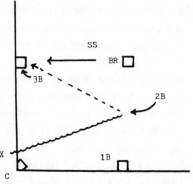

THE OUTFIELD

The first line of defense in softball is the infield. The second line of defense, or last defense, is the outfield. Any ball going through the outfield is a certain extra-base hit.

In general, outfielders must possess good running speed to cover the comparatively vast area for which they are responsible. The ability to accurately judge fly balls is also of prime importance. A strong accurate throwing arm, coupled with a thorough understanding of the game, rounds out the qualifications required of an outfielder.

The center fielder should possess the most speed and be the strongest all-round outfielder. Generally, the center fielder is regarded as the captain of the outfield, and as such, she should have a good understanding of the game itself. In plays where she must back up other outfielders, she will probably be the one to call the play that is to be made after the catch.

Since the majority of batters are right-handed, the left fielder receives many opportunities to test her skills. She must also possess good judgment of fly balls and a strong accurate arm. The right fielder is often the most neglected outfielder. However, it is the right fielder who has some of the most difficult balls to handle. Since most batters are right-handed, many of the balls hit to right field slice away from the outfielder. She must also know the game and react quickly—many a batter-baserunner is forced to stay at first base because a right fielder backed up an overthrow to first. The right fielder is the only outfielder who throws to first base to attempt a force out. This play is only possible if the right fielder is alert and is a good fielder with an accurate arm.

The basic techniques of catching fly balls make up the starting point for the outfielder. Once these fundamentals have been mastered, they are adjusted and adapted to suit the particular demands of the outfielder.

Instead of running to the point where she can intercept the downward path of a fly ball, a good outfielder will head for a point about 4 or 5 feet behind that anticipated point of interception. Then, as the ball is coming within her range, the outfielder will take one or two steps into the ball as she makes the catch. In this manner, with her body in motion on the catch, she quickly adjusts her feet and completes her throw with her momentum adding to the strength of her throw.

The overhand throw is the bread-and-butter throw of an outfielder. When distance, strength, and accuracy of the throw are vital, the overhand throw wins hands down over the sidearm technique. Also, since the vast majority of an outfielder's catches are made above shoulder level, it is natural for the automatic "giving" motion of the glove hand to bring the caught ball directly to the throwing shoulder—the starting point for the overhand throw.

All throws made by an outfielder should have a low trajectory. Although a throw with some arc to it may go farther, it is also slower. The bounce from such a throw is slower because it will be high. On the other hand, a low trajectory throw may bounce a little sooner, but the bounce is lower, more direct, and covers more distance. The low trajectory bounce is better for the infielder to handle because it comes in about knee or waist height, providing good position for a tag play.

For short distance throws by outfielders to infielders, direct line throws reaching the infielder without a bounce are preferred. The farther the throw, the more a bounce is preferred. Judging the point where the thrown ball should bounce depends upon the player making the throw. An outfielder with a strong arm, capable of throwing the ball at a high velocity, will utilize a bounce point further from the intended fielder than an outfielder whose throw has less velocity. Depending upon the velocity of the throw, the ball may bounce 10, 15, or 20 feet from the intended receiver. An important point to keep in mind when throwing the ball on a bounce is that a ball that bounces close to a fielder's feet is considered one of the hardest throws to handle.

One of the most difficult plays for an outfielder to

execute is the catching of a fly ball while running at full speed. Many an outfielder has made a spectacular run to reach a short fly ball over the infielder's reach only to have that ball bounce out of her glove. To counteract the force generated when two objects traveling toward each other meet, the ball must be contacted far enough in front of the body to enable the glove hand to relax or "give" on contact. If the ball is caught very close to the body, where the fielder cannot permit the glove to "give," the ball is more likely to bounce out of the glove.

By running on the balls of the feet, instead of on the heels and toes, the outfielder will find the ball easier to follow. The jouncing of the body caused by heel-toe running causes the ball to appear to bounce in the air and thus adds to the difficulty in accurately judging the interception point. When chasing down that long fly ball hit over her head, the outfielder must turn her back on the infield and run toward the interception point. When she runs away from the infield, whether on a diagonal or straight back, she should turn her head in order to look over her shoulder and keep the ball in view at all times. Occasionally, an outfielder will see a ball that she just knows is hit a country mile and will make an instant estimate of the possible interception point and head for it, disregarding the ball. An outfielder running in this fashion can probably run faster than her counterpart who keeps her eye on the ball, and thus may be able to reach a ball that the other cannot. However, this technique is dangerous for two reasons. One, by not keeping sight of the ball, an outfielder could overrun it and be hit by it. Two, no matter how good the outfielder is at estimating the interception point for the fly ball, the wind could cause it to be held up or blown slightly to the right or left, and the outfielder is then in danger of missing the ball completely.

The way in which an outfielder plays a ground ball varies depending upon the situation and the type of ground ball. If the ground ball is a slow one, the outfielder will play it in much the same manner as an infielder, the only difference being that the outfielder must charge in to field the slow ground ball. Failure to do so would probably result in the baserunner advancing an extra base. If the ground ball is well hit, the outfielder, being the last line of defense, should utilize her body to block the ball. The outfielder must first line up with the ball and move into position. Once in position, the outfielder drops down onto one knee, thus placing her body in a position to stop any ball that may ricochet off or bounce under her glove. Depending upon the path of the ball, the knee closest to the ball will be the one on which the outfielder will kneel.

If the situation is such at the time the ground ball is hit that the baserunner or runners will advance that one base and no further, the outfielder should play the ball safely by blocking its path with her body. On the other hand, if the winning run could score on that ground ball if it is not quickly returned to the infield to record an out, the outfielder must play the ball accordingly. In this situation, the outfielder should run in, field the grounder off her left foot (right-handed player), step right as the ball is brought up to the starting point of the throw, then step left and throw. The danger in this technique is that an erratic bounce by the ball may cause it to go past the outfielder's glove. However, if the winning run scores while the ground ball is being blocked, the game is also lost.

Probably most of the balls handled by outfielders are hit between players rather than directly to a specific player. When two players are running for the same ball, it becomes imperative that they call for the ball. A simple "mine," "got it," "take it," etc., will enable one player to make the catch safely and without interference while the second player can cut behind to be in a position to help if the first fielder has trouble handling the ball. The "take it" or "yours" are just as important, if not more so, than the initial "got it." If two players call for the ball, one must acquiesce to the other. Generally, an outfielder coming in on the ball takes precedence over an infielder running out. Also, among the three outfielders, the center fielder's call takes priority over that of either the right or left fielder.

Outfield Drills (See also Drill Key on page 21)

Drill #1. The coach (X) hits routine fly balls to the outfielder. The outfielder catches the fly ball and throws, with a low trajectory, from right field to third base on one bounce. (See diagram.) A cone, extra base, or glove can be utilized initially as a target to help the thrower

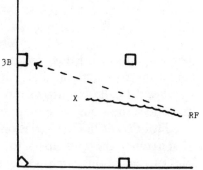

gauge the point at which her particular throw should hit the ground to obtain the desired low bounce to third. The target can be placed about 20 feet from the base and then adjusted to the individual's throw.

Drill #2. Coach 1 (X₁) fungo hits fly balls to the left fielder, who catches them and throws to the third baseman on the fly. Coach 2 (X₂) fungo hits fly balls to the center fielder, who catches them and throws to the second baseman on the fly. Coach 3 (X₃) fungo hits fly balls to the right

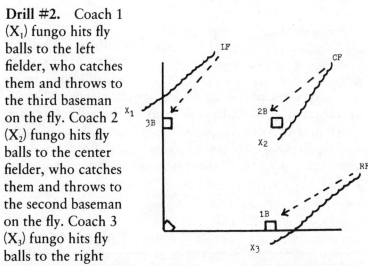

fielder, who catches them and throws to the first baseman on the fly. One player can be in each outfield position, or there can be a line of three or four who rotate positions. (See diagram.)

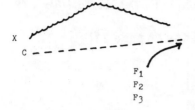

Drill #3. Standing about 100 feet from a line of fielders, the coach (X) hits fly balls a distance of about 120 to 140 feet. When ball number one is hit, Outfielder 1 turns her back toward the coach and runs to catch the ball hit over her head. After she catches the ball, she throws it to the catcher. Each fielder in turn does the same. (See diagram.) Three variations can be used for this drill. One variation is for the coach to hit balls that require the outfielders to run diagonally back to the right to make the catch. Other balls can be hit so that the fielders have to run diagonally back and toward the left. In a third variation, balls can be hit directly over the fielder's head. In all instances, the balls should be hit with sufficient loft to enable the fielders to actually catch most of the fly balls.

Drill #4. Here the coach (X) fungo hits fly balls to a small group of three to five outfielders standing about 10 to 15 feet apart. The outfielders must call for the ball before they catch it. If two call for the ball simultaneously, one should call out "take it" or "yours" to avoid any confusion. After the catch, the ball is thrown back to the catcher. (See diagram.)

THE FORCE PLAY

A force play is one in which the baserunner does not have to be tagged in order to be out. When a batter hits a ground ball, she must run to first base. If the ball is fielded and thrown to the first baseman, who tags the base while in possession of the ball before that batter-baserunner reaches first base, the batter-baserunner is forced out. When a batter hits a ground ball with a runner on first base, that runner on first base loses the right to that base by the fact that the batter becomes a baserunner and, therefore, must vacate first and try to advance to second. The same is true with runners on first and second or first, second, and third when the batter hits a ground ball, since each is forced to vacate her base because of the baserunner directly behind.

THE DOUBLE PLAY

A double play is a situation where two outs are obtained on a play initiated by one batted or pitched ball. They come in a wide variety of combinations.

The most common double plays involve the shortstop, second and first basemen of the defensive team. Two other elements involved are (1) the batter hits a ground ball, and (2) there is a runner on first base. If the ground ball is fielded by the shortstop, she tosses the ball to the second baseman covering second, who tags second base to force out the runner going to second and then throws on to first base to force out the batter-baserunner. Another common form of the double play occurs when a ground ball is fielded by the second baseman, who throws to the shortstop covering second to force out the baserunner. The shortstop then throws on to first base to record the second force out. A third form of the double play occurs when the first baseman fields a ground ball and throws to the shortstop covering second, who in turn throws back to first base, where either the first baseman or second baseman takes the return throw for the second force out.

Double plays can also be initiated by the catcher, pitcher, or third baseman. If there are runners on first and second, and the ground ball is hit near third, the third baseman can field the ball, run to and tag her base for the first out, and then throw to first for the second out. In a bases loaded situation, the first play is at home to force out the lead runner, then the second out is recorded at first. In these ways the advance runner becomes the first out.

Another variety of double play involves a caught line drive with a runner or runners on base. Since a baserunner must return to her base after a fly ball has been caught before she can advance, it is possible to catch that runner off her base if she has taken a large enough lead. In this situation, the infielder who caught the line drive merely has to throw the ball to another fielder covering the base that the runner vacated. If the fielder covering the vacated base tags that base while in possession of the ball, before the runner can return, the second out is recorded.

There is another version of the double play initiated by a caught fly ball. In situations where the batter hits a fly ball to the outfield when the offensive team has a run and hit play on, the outfielder, after the catch, may be able to throw to the base that the runner vacated before that runner can return.

Double Play Drills (See also Drill Key on Page 21)

Drill #1. Start with a shortstop, second baseman, first baseman, and catcher. The coach (X) calls the play—"go for two"—and then hits a ground ball to the shortstop. The shortstop fields the ground ball and throws it to the second baseman covering second. The second baseman tags second with her foot and throws on to the first baseman covering first. The first baseman then throws to the catcher. (See diagram.)

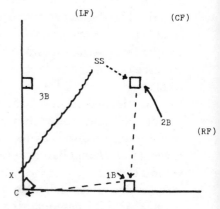

When ground balls are hit to the second baseman and first baseman, the shortstop covers second for the throw and relays the ball to first base. After the shortstop–second base combination takes shape, a third baseman (E) may be added to the practice. Then, a ground ball may be hit to the third baseman, who fields the ball and throws to the second baseman covering second. The second baseman again relays the throw to first base for the second out.

Ground balls can be hit, in order, to the third baseman, the shortstop, the second baseman, and the first baseman. However, since developing timing between the second baseman and shortstop is vital to the development of a double play combination, ground balls involving these two players should receive priority.

Drill #2. The coach (X) calls a base where an imaginary runner is located and then fungo hits soft line drives to the infielders. After an infielder has caught the line drive, she throws the ball to the base indicated by the coach in an attempt to double up the imaginary baserunner. (See diagram.)

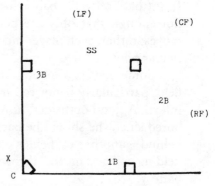

Baserunners can be added once the infielders are familiar with the type of play. If baserunners are added, some of the line drives should intentionally be hit through the infield to keep the baserunners honest. Outfielders can also be utilized to back up hits and throws.

Drill #3. The coach (X) calls a base and fungo hits fly balls to the outfield. The outfielder catches the ball, then

quickly throws it to
the base indicated by
the coach to double up
the imaginary
baserunner. (See
diagram.) If
baserunners are added,
some base hits must be
intentionally hit to
ensure that the
baserunners take
honest leads.

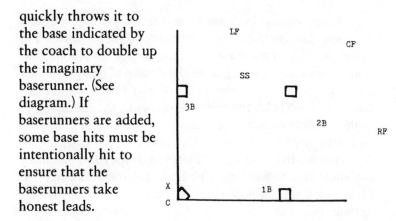

BACKING UP

In softball, once the ball is hit, everyone should move. It is
not enough that only the player to whom the ball is hit
moves; rather, each player must move in relation to the particular play.

Some players are bored if they are "stuck" in the outfield, particularly if not too many balls are hit beyond the
infield. A good outfielder, however, doesn't have time to be
bored since she should be backing up—that is, running in
behind—another outfielder on the batted ball, an infielder
fielding a ball, or the throws made by infielders or the
battery.

In addition to fielding all fly and ground balls hit to
her, the left fielder should also back up the shortstop and
third baseman when balls are hit to those two infielders.
Although the batter-baserunner will be safe at first base if
the ball goes through the shortstop or third baseman, if the
left fielder is there to pick up the ball a few feet behind the
infielder, the baserunner will remain at first, or can be
thrown out if she attempts to advance beyond first. Any
time that the catcher throws to third base, either to cut
down a runner attempting to steal third or to pick off a
baserunner, the left fielder should back up the throw. Mov-

ing into foul ground behind third base, in line with a throw from first base, is another back-up responsibility of the left fielder.

A left fielder should also back up the center fielder on all balls hit to center and left center. Also, if a baserunner is caught between third and second, the left fielder, if she lines up with the play in foul ground, can help prevent the possibility of the baserunner scoring if she gets past the third baseman or of the throw getting past the third baseman. (See diagram.)

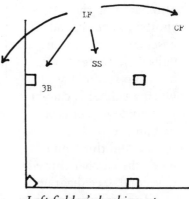

Left fielder's backing up responsibilities

On the other side of the outfield, the right fielder has similar responsibilities. Besides playing all balls hit to right field, she backs up both the first baseman and the second baseman on all of their plays. If the catcher attempts to pick off a runner on first base, the right fielder should back up the throw in case it is off target and thus prevent that baserunner from advancing. A good right fielder will back up first base on all throws from the left side of the field and when plays are being made on a runner caught between first and second bases. She also backs up the center fielder on all balls hit to center and right center. (See diagram.)

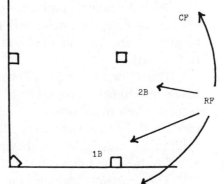

Right fielder's backing up responsibilities

The center fielder backs up both the right and left fielders on all balls hit to them. She also backs up the shortstop and second baseman on all ground balls. The center fielder backs up second base when a runner is caught in a rundown between first and second or second and third, and when the catcher throws to second. (See diagram.)

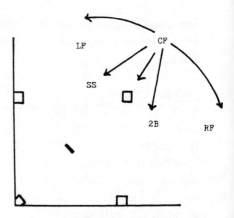

Center fielder's backing up responsibilities

Infielders and the battery also share in backing up one another. On throws to home and third base from the out-field, the pitcher goes into foul ground, in line with the throw, to back up the catcher and third baseman. If the catcher is drawn away from the home plate area by an off target throw, or if the first baseman is pulled too far to her right to field a ball, the pitcher may actually cover home plate or first base, respectively. The pitcher may also cover third base on plays where the third baseman is pulled away from third, such as on fielding a bunt.

With no runners on base, or perhaps with only a runner on first base, the catcher will run down, in foul ground, to back up first base on all plays that could result in throws to first base.

The second baseman (2B) backs up first when the first baseman (1B) fields ground balls to her right and backs up second when the shortstop is taking the throw from the catcher. If the first baseman is pulled in, for example, when fielding a bunt, the second baseman covers first base. She also covers second on ground balls hit to the left side.

The shortstop backs up the third baseman on ground balls and the second baseman when she covers second. She also covers second base on ground balls to the right side and when a runner attempts to steal second. Both the short-stop and the second baseman are always on the alert to pick up any overthrown balls to the pitcher.

Backing Up Drills (See also Drill Key on page 21)

Drill #1. The coach (X) calls the play at either third or home and then fungo hits balls to the outfield. If the ball is hit to the center fielder, both the right and left fielders should move to back her up. After the center fielder catches the ball, she throws to the base specified by the coach, and the pitcher backs up either third or home, depending upon the play. A similar procedure is followed when balls are hit to left and right field. (See diagram.)

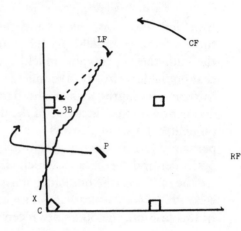

Drill #2. The coach fungo hits balls to the first baseman. The second baseman cuts behind the first baseman to back her up and the pitcher moves to cover first. The first base-man calls if she thinks that she is capable of handling the play without any assistance; otherwise, she tosses the ball to the pitcher covering first.

RELAY SYSTEMS

Although a ball can cover greater distances if it is thrown with an upward trajectory, this also consumes valuable time. A ball thrown on a line—that is, parallel to the ground—utilizing a relay composed of two or three players will cover an equal distance faster than a ball thrown by one individual that must first ascend and then descend from an apex. Therefore, when a batted ball is hit over an outfielder's head, or between two outfielders, a relay system is used to return the ball to the infield in the shortest possible time.

The usual relay players are the shortstop, for throws from left and center field, and the second baseman, for throws from right field. As the outfielder is chasing down the ball, the appropriate infielder moves partway toward that outfielder. How far the infielder goes depends upon the throwing strength of both the particular outfielder's arm and her own arm. Since one of the desirable attributes of an outfielder is a strong throwing arm, the infielder moves out perhaps 20 or 30 feet and positions herself in line with the outfielder and the base to which she anticipates the throw will be made. As the outfielder starts to pick up the ball, the relay player starts to call and raise her arms above her head. In this fashion, the outfielder receives both a visible and an

Calling for the ball on a relay.
*The infielder, with her arms
extended upward, calls for the
ball.*

audible signal on which to home in. The sooner the outfielder knows where to throw the ball, the sooner she can start it back to the infield.

Because a relay player is being utilized, the outfielder can save precious seconds because she does not have to build momentum for the throw by taking several steps. Instead, she should try to shift her weight onto her right foot (for a right-handed outfielder) as she picks up the ball. Then, as she comes up, she can pivot on her right foot in order to step toward the relay player with her left foot as she throws. With the throw on its way, the relay player should turn sideways, with her glove side closer to the infield, to line up exactly with the incoming throw. If the incoming throw is strong enough, the relay player can be moving sideways toward the infield as she catches the ball in front of her body. When she catches the ball, she quickly takes it in her throwing hand and, utilizing the momentum she has already built up, takes one additional step with her left foot (right-handed player) and throws to the appropriate base.

Since outfielders generally possess strong throwing arms, another outfielder rather than an infielder could become the relay player. In plays involving balls hit between two outfielders, the two have to make a fairly quick determination as to which outfielder will continue to chase down the ball. This decision is based upon which outfielder has the better position to reach the ball as quickly as possible. Once this decision has been made, the other outfielder can then position herself in line with the "chasing" outfielder and the base most likely to be the target of the throw.

Utilizing a second outfielder instead of an infielder may have several advantages. The outfielder is best prepared to effect throws from the outfield to home plate on one bounce. In pregame warmups, while infielders make their throws to the bases on the fly, the outfielders make their practice throws to the bases on a bounce. Thus, the outfielder already has a mental target area for the particular field surface. A second advantage of this method is that the infielder can back up the throw to the outfielder–relay player, thus minimizing the danger of a possible overthrow. A third advantage is that the infielder can call the play for the relay player to execute. Since that infielder does not have to keep her eye on the thrown ball as constantly as the actual relay player, she can more accurately perceive the best possible play. Also, since the infielder does not signal for a throw but merely calls the best play as the relay player is lining up with the first throw, there should be no confusion as to the player with whom the outfielder is working.

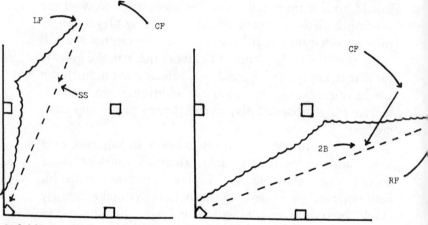

Infielder as a relay player   *Outfielder as a relay player*

Which of the two methods should be employed depends upon the skills of the individual team members. A team may have outfielders who catch extremely well but have less than optimum throwing power or accuracy. In this situation, using the infielders as relay players may be the most beneficial method for the team as a whole. If, on the other hand, a team's outfielders possess strong accurate throwing arms, using a second outfielder as the relay player may be more advantageous. In either case, for the relay system to be successful, that first outfielder who initiates the relay has to be able to hit the relay player.

Relay System Drills (See also Drill Key on page 21)

Drill #1. Player 1 throws a long fly ball to Player 2, who catches the ball and throws, on a line, to the relay player, who is positioned on the line between them. As Player 1 throws to Player 2, the relay player turns sideways and lines up between Player 1 and the ball. The relay player catches the throw from Player 2, takes one step, and throws to Player 1. The distance separating Players 1 and 2 and the relay player depends on the players' throwing ability and whether practice is indoors or outdoors.

Drill #2. The coach (X) fungo hits balls to an outfielder (F_1), who catches the ball and throws to the relay player (RP). The relay player throws to the catcher. F_1 turns and goes to the end of the line and the drill is repeated with each outfielder. (See diagram.)

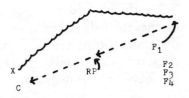

Drill #3. With one outfielder (F_1) in a ready position, line up other outfielders 10 or more feet behind her. The coach (X) hits the ball past the outfielder, who chases it down and throws it to the shortstop, who has positioned herself in line with home plate. The shortstop completes the throw to the catcher on one bounce. The drill is repeated with each fielder. (See diagram.) The drill can be

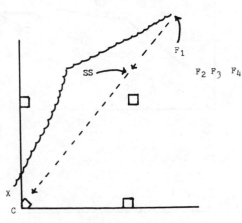

varied by utilizing the second baseman as the relay player for outfielders in right field.

Drill #4. The team is set up on the field with the coach (X) hitting fungos between outfielders or over their heads. The coach calls the play (i.e., home, third, etc.) and hits the ball. The outfielder catches the ball and looks for the relay player to throw to. While the outfielder catches the ball, either

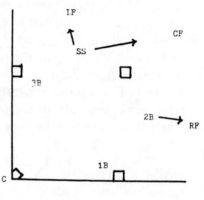

the shortstop or second baseman positions herself for a relay throw. The relay is made to the appropriate base by the infielder. (See diagram.)

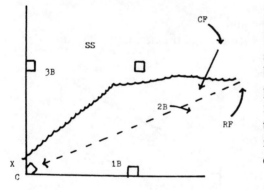

Drill #5. As in Drill #4, but the second outfielder becomes the relay player and the infielder becomes the assistant to the relay player. (See diagram.)

THE CUT-OFF

Closely associated with the relay is the cut-off. The cut-off play generally involves the first baseman and becomes an important factor when one or more runners have scored and others are still on the base paths. The cut-off player is the first baseman. In this capacity, she positions herself between home plate and the pitcher's plate, about 10 or 15 feet from the pitcher's plate. The cut-off player must be far enough in front of the catcher so that she does not block the catcher's view of the ball. Depending upon which direction the throw is coming from, the first baseman, often with the help of the catcher, will move to her right or left to maintain alignment with the ball and home plate.

Although the cut-off player is the first baseman, the decision to cut or not to cut the throw belongs to the catcher. The catcher is in the best position to observe the baserunners and to assess the possibility of a successful play at home plate. If the runner is too close to home plate for a possible play or has crossed the plate, the catcher should call "cut"; the catcher may also call the base where she sees a possible play. If the call to cut is not heard, the first baseman should quickly step to the side, away from the throw, to permit the catcher a better view of the incoming throw.

When executed properly, the cut-off can result in successful plays on baserunners who otherwise would be permitted to advance an extra base. If executed improperly, the results can be disastrous. The decision to attempt the cut-off play depends upon the level of play and the abilities of the catcher and first baseman. The more experienced the players, the better the chances for success. However, it is vital that the catcher have the experience, knowledge, and judgment to make the calls early enough and loudly enough to avoid confusion. The catcher and first baseman must have confidence in the other's ability. Failure of this teamwork may result in a cut-off player who backs up into the catcher or who takes it upon herself to decide to cut a throw that the catcher felt would have prevented a run from scoring. Lack of teamwork not only permits runs to score, but also results in frustrated ball players.

A possible alternative to the common cut-off play is to give the catcher the prerogative to cut the throw if she feels the possibility of a play at home is useless. By providing a back-up for the catcher—either the pitcher or first baseman —and depending upon the play, the catcher will be in a position to move out in front of the plate when she deems it appropriate. This last option might be considerably less confusing for less experienced players.

Cut-Off Drills (See also Drill Key on page 21)

Drill #1. The coach (X) fungo hits balls to the outfielders one at a time. The first outfielder (F₁) steps away from the line and plays the first batted ball. After she catches the ball, she throws it to the catcher at home plate. If the ball is to be cut, the catcher calls "cut"

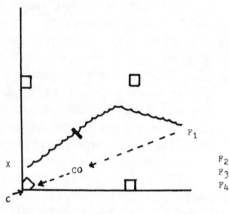

and the cut-off player (CO) catches the ball and then relays it to the catcher with an easy toss. If no call to cut is made, the cut-off player steps to the side, away from the throw. (See diagram.) This drill provides the opportunity for the catcher and first baseman to develop teamwork and gives the outfielders varied practice.

Drill #2. Once the basic teamwork of the cut-off play has been mastered, a full team is utilized. All throws from the outfield are made to home plate. The coach (X) fungo hits balls to the outfielders. The first baseman moves into the cut-off position, and with the aid of the catcher she lines up for the play. The second and third basemen cover their respective bases. If the catcher calls "cut," she follows that call with a base designation. The first baseman cuts the

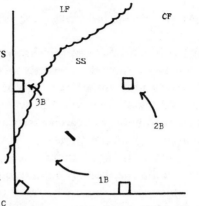

throw, and in turn throws to the base designated by the catcher. If no call is made, the first baseman steps to the side and permits the throw to go through to the catcher. (See diagram.)

Drill #3. The fielders are set up as in Drill #2; however, a pitcher may be added to back up home plate. The main difference is the fact that baserunners are added at first and third. The baserunners try to legally score or advance on each batted ball. The decision to cut or not to cut must now be made in relation to actual baserunners. A batter-baserunner and a runner on second may be added as the expertise of the fielders increases.

THE RUNDOWN

The rundown of a runner caught between two bases is an important defensive play. This play may involve two, three, or more defensive players. Since these players must be careful to avoid contact with the runner, unless making a tag, more than four players can interfere with the success of the play.

The fielder with the ball should run straight at the baserunner, holding the ball about head height in her throwing hand. With the ball in this position, should the runner commit herself to running toward the other base, the fielder is able to make a quick snap throw to the other fielder, using the wrist and forearm instead of a large wind-up. It is safer to keep the throws on the inside of the base path since throwing directly over the runner may easily result in a hit runner or a high or lofted throw. The fielders should try to keep the throws approximately at shoulder height to make the catch easier and to enable the fielder to maintain good position.

Once the baserunner is caught between two fielders, two additional fielders should join the play as back-ups. If the play is in progress between first and second bases, the pitcher or catcher may go over to cover first base in case either the runner or ball gets past the first baseman. At the same time, the shortstop may come in to second base to back up on that side of the play. Should the runner get past the first baseman during the rundown play, the first baseman must be careful to quickly get out of the runner's way to avoid contact. As the first baseman is taking herself out of the play, the throw can be made to the back-up fielder covering first for a possible tag of the runner or continuation of the play. Once the first baseman has taken herself out of the immediate action, she should assume the role of the back-up fielder. She may assume the back-up role by replacing the fielder who took over for her, or continue on and back up the other side of the play. It is very important for the fielder no longer involved in the play to take herself out of the base path in order to avoid an interference call. Although the defensive team is usually the victor, if the runner cannot be tagged out, she should at least be forced to return to the base she left.

If there is another runner on base at this time, her actions must also be monitored by the defensive team. Should the defensive team be successful and tag out the runner caught in the rundown, the fielder who made the tag must be ready to make a play on that second runner. In this situation, the fielder making the tag should touch the runner with the back of the glove, using the throwing hand to help hold on to the ball by squeezing the glove shut. Also, as the tag is made, the fielder should "give" and step back and away, out of the runner's path.

Rundown Drills

Drill #1. Player 1, with the ball in her throwing hand, stands in front of second base. Player 2 stands in front of first base, holding her glove up about shoulder high as a target. Player 1 runs forward, holding the ball up. As she runs forward, she may fake a throw once or twice before actually throwing to Player 2. After the throw, Player 1 continues her forward movement, going to the rear of a line of players behind first, being careful to stay far enough to the right to avoid any contact. (See diagram.)

After the catch, Player 2 moves forward toward Player 3, who has stepped in front of the base. Player 2 fakes a throw or two before she actually throws the ball, and then continues to the end of the line behind second. Players continue to shuttle back and forth.

Drill #2. Two bases are set up 60 feet apart, with Players 1 and 2 as basemen and Player 3 as the baserunner. Player 3 is on Player 1's base. Player 1 throws the ball to 2, and 3 leaves the base and starts toward the other base. Player 2 runs directly toward 3, trying to tag her or force her to try to return to the base she left. If Player 2 forces the runner to attempt to return to the base, Player 2 throws the ball to 1. Then Player 1 attempts to tag the runner. Players 1 and 2 take turns running at the runner, attempting to tag her. The drill is continued until either the runner is tagged out or until she reaches a base safely. The same baserunner may be used for succeeding trials, or the baserunner can rotate with the basemen.

BUNT SITUATIONS

Generally, when the defensive team anticipates that the offensive team may bunt, things begin to happen in the infield. A possible bunt is communicated through the use of signals or verbally, and the defensive team prepares to handle a bunt, should it materialize.

If hand signals are used, the preparation by the defensive team may go unnoticed by the offensive team. Then, if the offensive team executes the suspected bunt, the defensive team is ready to handle the situation. If, on the other hand, verbal communication is used, everyone will know that the defensive team is prepared for a possible bunt. In this situation, the offensive players may decide to change strategy because they have lost the element of surprise, or they may continue with the original strategy. If they keep the bunt on, the defensive team has succeeded in placing more pressure on the batter because once the batter knows that the opposition is ready, she also knows that her bunt must be perfect in order to be successful. The offensive players may also decide to continue with the planned bunt because they believe the communication was merely an attempt by the defensive team to cause them to shy away from the bunt.

Regardless of whether signals or verbal communication is utilized to alert the defensive team, changes must be made to accommodate the possibility of handling a bunt situation. The third and first basemen and the battery are the four defensive players involved in fielding bunted balls. As the pitcher takes her place on the pitcher's plate, the first and third basemen cheat a little by taking two or three steps in toward home plate before getting into a ready position. Both will charge in toward home plate with the pitch. By charging the plate, they not only decrease the amount of time between the time the ball is bunted and the time it is fielded, but they also intimidate the batter. Because of her good fielding position, a competent third baseman may field all bunts toward third, as well as those toward the pitcher, and even bunts a little on the first base side of the pitcher's area. The reason for this responsibility is that as she fields the bunt, her momentum is carrying her toward first base, where most plays on bunted balls will be handled. Both the first and third basemen have the advantage of being able to approach simultaneously with the pitch, whereas the pitcher must first release the pitch and the catcher must stay in position to catch the pitch should the batter not bunt the ball.

Although the catcher must wait until the ball is actually bunted before she can charge out to field the bunt, she is in an excellent position to throw to any base. The catcher's body position is open to all bases, and her momentum is in the same general direction as her throw, whereas both the first baseman and the pitcher must stop and turn before making any throw.

The pitcher's role in fielding bunts depends upon the ability of the other three players. If the first and third basemen and catcher are experienced and capable, they will probably reach the bunted ball faster than the pitcher. With less experienced players, however, the pitcher will handle the major share of bunted balls by charging in after the pitch is released.

Although the second baseman and shortstop do not field bunted balls, they are vital links in the success of any bunt defense. In a suspected bunt situation, the second baseman will cover first base to take the throw after the bunt has been fielded. This eliminates both the confusion as to who will cover first base and the necessity for the first baseman to reverse her forward momentum and try to return to first to take the throw from the catcher, pitcher, or third baseman. The shortstop moves to cover second base, making a play possible if the bunter attempts to advance to second. Also, if a runner is on first base at the time of the bunt, the shortstop will be ready to receive a throw attempting a play on the lead runner. If there is a runner on second base at the time of the bunt, the shortstop may go directly to third to cover that base, thus setting up a play on the lead runner.

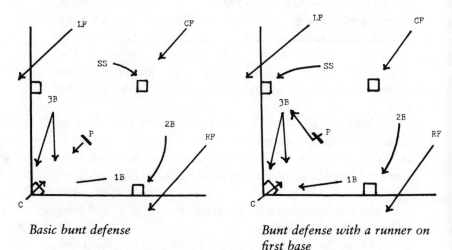

Basic bunt defense

Bunt defense with a runner on first base

Covering third base is an important aspect of bunt defense. Even with a runner on first base at the time of the bunt, most plays are still made to first to get the bunter-baserunner. Because of the greater distance of a throw to second base, and the fact that the baserunner has left with the release of the pitch, it is very difficult to record the out at second. Therefore, the runner on first base will often go to second base on the bunt and attempt to reach third while the play is being made on the bunter-baserunner, particularly if third is left uncovered. Because the third baseman is the prime bunt fielder, it is usually quite difficult for her to return to third in time to catch the throw. Generally, the pitcher will cover third. Usually, just the fact that a player is covering the base is enough to deter a baserunner from trying to stretch for third in a bunt situation. An alternative is to have the catcher continue her forward momentum and cover third. She has the advantage of being accustomed to making tag plays. If the catcher covers third, then either the pitcher or first baseman must continue in to cover home plate, or both may continue toward home, with the pitcher assuming her normal back-up role while the first baseman takes home plate.

Although infielders handle all bunted balls, the outfielders also react to a bunt situation. They assume their ready positions several steps in toward the infield as the pitcher gets set to pitch. As the ball is bunted, they charge in to assume back-up roles. The left fielder will back up throws to third and sometimes she may also cover third base, although she must travel the farthest. The right fielder backs up all throws to first base, and the center fielder backs up second.

Very often, the ball is intentionally bunted down the first or third base line. Such balls may hug the foul line, or may alternately roll fair and foul depending upon the pitch of the field. This type of bunt tests the ability of the fielder to quickly assess the situation. If the fielder is caught off guard by the bunt and realizes that she does not have a play on the bunter-baserunner, she may allow the ball to roll, hoping it will go foul. The instant it rolls foul, the fielder should touch it with her glove, hand, or foot, since once a ball is touched in foul ground it is ruled a foul ball. If, however, the fielder sees that the bunter has given the ball up for a foul and has stopped running toward first, she should follow the ball and be ready to pick it up the instant it enters fair ground. If the ball does roll fair before reaching either first or third, she will have an easy play on the bunter-baserunner.

Many bunted balls are fielded in the same manner as any other ground ball, except that the fielder throws without first straightening up. Bunted balls which are slowly rolling or bouncing are sometimes picked up by the fielder with her throwing hand, thereby eliminating the transfer from glove to hand and saving precious time. Occasionally, a bunted ball has a great amount of spin, which makes it difficult to "find the handle." When a bunted ball is spinning, just using the glove to smother the ball will kill the spin and enable the fielder to handle the ball cleanly.

Bunt Drills

Bunt defense can be practiced first with the infielders alone and the coach bunting the ball. As the infielders master the techniques of who fields the ball and who covers the base, first one, then a second baserunner may be added to the practice.

FIRST AND THIRD SITUATIONS

One of the most frustrating situations for inexperienced defensive teams is the one that arises with runners on first and third. If the runner on first base breaks for second and the defensive team plays her, the runner from third may score. Or worse, if the throw is wild, both runners may score. If the defensive team merely permits the runner on first to advance to second, the chance for a double play is lost and two runners will be in scoring position.

Once the infielders are capable of throwing accurately, there are several choices. One option is for the catcher to throw the ball to third base in the hope of catching the lead runner unaware and expecting to see a play at second. Either the third baseman or shortstop can cover third on such a play. If the third baseman covers third, the shortstop backs up the throw. Should the shortstop cover third, the left fielder would provide the back-up.

A second option would be to have the catcher fake a throw to second and then actually throw to third. Or, the catcher could fake a throw to second by executing a hard throw to the pitcher. If the fake is successful, the pitcher has the option to play the runner who is caught off-base. The advantage in this option, particularly for an inexperienced team, is that the throw is short and the ball remains in the center of the infield area. Depending on assigned base coverage, either the shortstop or second baseman, as well as the center fielder, should back up the throw to the pitcher. Of course, there is also the option of the catcher attempting to pick off the runner at first base. This is a poor choice because the throw is made behind the runner and that would encourage the runner to advance to second.

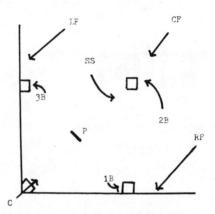

Backing up in a first and third situation

For more experienced teams, the shortstop can move into position midway between the pitcher's plate and second base, in line with home and second. After the catcher catches the pitch, she immediately cocks her throwing arm, checks the runner at third, and, if that runner is not playable, fires the ball to second. The throw must be hard and low, going directly to the base. Because of the trajectory of the throw, the pitcher must duck. If the runner on third heads home on the throw, the catcher calls "cut" and the shortstop catches the throw and plays the runner going home from third. If the runner at third stays put, the shortstop permits the throw to go through to the second baseman for a tag play at second. Whatever the first play, the team must remain aware of the activities of the other baserunner. Of course, the first and third basemen must cover their respective bases and be ready for a possible play. Should the runner from first not continue on to second, a rundown may evolve. Although the action involves the infielders, it is necessary for the outfielders to position themselves to back up any wide throws. Again, the left fielder assumes responsibility for backing up third; the right fielder, first; and the center fielder, second.

Batting

The batter must be aggressive and want to hit that pitched ball. Instead of waiting for the "perfect" pitch, the batter should feel confident enough to go after any pitch in the strike zone. A batter capable of hitting both inside and outside pitches is more of a threat to the defensive team than the batter who hits only inside pitches. It is more difficult for the pitcher to throw successfully against an aggressive hitter who will swing at and hit any ball thrown than against a batter who waits for "her" pitch. A batter who is determined to wait for her pitch may have a long wait if the opposing pitcher learns what her pitch is. Although a batter should be aggressive at the plate, she should not be overanxious to swing at anything thrown by the pitcher.

To become a batter who is able to discriminate between good and bad pitches takes a lot of batting practice and the ability to concentrate on the pitched ball. Regardless of the wind-up utilized by the pitcher, the batter must have the self-discipline to concentrate on the pitcher's release point, which is usually in the vicinity of her knee or thigh. The batter should visually pick up the ball at the pitcher's release point and then follow that ball until it either contacts her bat or enters the catcher's glove.

The oft repeated adage "A walk is as good as a hit" can be harmful to a batter. A batter who intentionally looks for a walk can very quickly and frequently find herself on the short end of the count and called out by the umpire. If a batter is facing a pitcher for the first time, there is nothing wrong with making that pitcher throw a pitch or two in order to adjust to a different style of pitching. Also, if the pitcher is incapable of locating the plate, common sense dictates waiting and not rushing to swing. Knowing the strike zone and having the ability to classify the pitch instantly as a ball or strike are important to a batter's success. Whether or not a batter's judgment of the pitch is the same as that of the umpire is something else. Remember, every pitch in the vicinity of a corner of the plate that is ruled a strike by the umpire leaves a happy pitcher and an unhappy batter, and for every pitch ruled a ball, the reverse is true.

Once the batter has an idea of what is expected, the first order of business is the selection of a bat. The bat chosen should be the heaviest bat available that the batter is able to use without any ill effects on the mechanics of her swing. If the bat is too light, she will be robbed of her power potential. If the bat is too heavy, her bat control will be affected and her swing will be poor and late. The stronger the batter's wrists and upper body, the heavier the bat that she will be able to control. It is important for the batter to feel comfortable and confident when swinging the bat of her choice.

TECHNIQUES

The mechanics of the swing, contact, and follow-through as described here provide the foundation for all batters.

However, it is important that each batter feel comfortable with her own stance, swing, and follow-through. Therefore, there are many slight variations of the basics.

There are three classifications of grip: the long or power grip, the choke or short grip, and the regular grip. The long grip, where the batter's lower hand (the left hand for a right-handed batter) is close to the knob end of the bat, is used by power hitters. This grip provides the best leverage and can add to the power and distance achieved by a batter with good bat control. The choke grip, where the lower hand is placed about 5 or 6 inches above the knob end of the bat, provides the greatest amount of bat control. In return for greater control of the bat, the batter gives up power. The regular grip, where the batter's lower hand is about 2 or 3 inches from the knob end of the bat, permits good bat control and considerable power. Regardless of the length of the grip, the top hand (the right hand for a right-handed batter) is placed directly next to or above the lower hand. When the top hand is placed on the bat, the knuckles should line up so that the second and third joints of the little

Gripping the bat. *The hands should be together, knuckles aligned.*

finger of the top hand rest directly between the second and third joints of the index finger of the lower hand. When the knuckles are aligned, the fingers are wrapped around the handle. The bat is gripped only by the fingers and upper palm and is not held down in the lower palm area since this inhibits the swing mechanics. During the swing into the ball, on contact, and on the follow-through, the bat must be securely gripped. However, while waiting for the pitcher to pitch, loosening the fingers of the upper hand will help to relax the grip enough to relieve harmful tension that would interfere with a free swing.

The open, closed, and regular (or parallel) stances are the three types used in softball. In the open stance the front foot is farther from the plate than the rear foot, and the body of the batter is more open to the pitcher than in any other stance. The open stance also provides the batter with a better view of the pitched ball and enables her to swing faster. It is most helpful against a very fast pitcher and in hitting inside pitches. In the closed stance, the batter's front foot is closer to the plate than her rear foot and the back of her forward shoulder is turned slightly toward the pitcher. This stance is helpful in hitting outside pitches and in slowing down the speed of the batter's swing. In the regular stance, the feet are parallel. This is the most common stance; it permits the batter to step directly into the pitch, whether inside, outside, or down the middle.

The distance that a player stands from the plate varies with

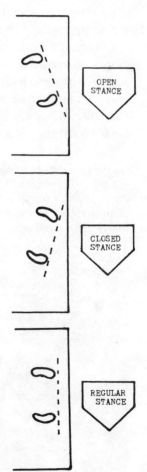

each individual. A general rule of thumb used to determine the best distance is to have the batter, after she has assumed her stance, extend her bat as in a swing to see that the widest part of it is over the plate. Whether the batter stands to the rear or in front of the batter's box depends mainly upon the opposing pitcher. If the pitcher is very fast, standing a little farther back affords a fraction of a second more to get the bat around to meet the ball. However, if the pitcher throws balls that break, standing in the front part of the batter's box can minimize the effect of a drop or rise by allowing the batter to hit the ball before it has the chance to drop or rise. Moving up in the box is also helpful against a slow pitcher.

Regardless of the stance chosen, the batter's weight should be evenly distributed on the balls of both feet as she waits for the pitch. Her knees and hips are slightly flexed. The feet should be approximately shoulder width apart. The batter's body is parallel to the side of home plate with the forward shoulder closest to the pitcher.

Batting stance. *The head faces the pitcher, the chin is tucked into the shoulder, and the elbows are away from the body; the bat is back.*

The swing. *Eyes must be on the ball. The forward foot steps toward the ball, the rear leg is bent, and the wrists lead the bat into the swing.*

Both arms are away from the body with the elbows flexed. The hands and elbows are about shoulder height, at the top of the strike zone, and the hands are behind the rear shoulder. Holding the arms away from the body permits an uninhibited swing. Starting with the hands at the top of the strike zone helps the batter to better judge high pitches. It also causes the batter to swing at a slightly downward angle to better meet a pitch that comes from a lower plane. The bat is extended back, pointing toward the backstop, almost parallel to the ground, as opposed to the vertical position used in baseball. The batter's head is turned toward the pitcher, with the chin tucked into the forward shoulder.

As the pitcher releases the ball, the batter's weight moves onto the rear foot, enabling her to step toward the pitch with her forward foot. The stride into the pitch should be about 10 to 15 inches in length. A longer stride may result in swinging under the ball. As the rear hip rotates forward, the weight transfers onto the forward foot.

Contact with the ball is made out in front as the wrists whip the bat around. Eyes are still on the ball.

The swing continues after the ball has been hit.

Both legs are bent at the knee, the rear leg close to a 90-degree angle and the front leg bent enough to keep the weight on the ball of the forward foot. The wrists lead the bat as the swing is started. With both wrists behind the bat, the head of the bat is whipped forward to contact the ball in front of the plate. On contact, the arms should be well away from the body. The swing continues, finishing with the bat somewhere in the vicinity of the center of the batter's back. Throughout the entire swing, the player's head remains stationary, the body rotating around it. The fixed position of the head enables the batter to follow the ball from the time it leaves the pitcher's hand until it meets the bat or goes into the catcher's glove.

Once a player has developed her stance, swing, and follow-through, the following pointers can be of assistance. While a batter is in the process of getting set in her stance, wiggling the hips, shoulders, and so on will have no ill effects on her batting. Once the batter has assumed her stance, however, she should remain still until she steps into the pitch. Wiggling the bat or body serves only to disrupt the smooth, fluid swing a batter works so hard to develop.

While the opposing pitcher takes her warm-up pitches and pitches to teammates, the offensive team members should spend some time studying her motion and strategy. It is sometimes possible to pick up little things that tip off her next pitch or to discover a pattern to her pitching. Sometimes a pitcher changes her motion slightly for a particular pitch or repeats a successful order of pitches, such as inside on the hands, then low outside, and so on. If a batter has some idea of what pitch is coming, it is easier to be ready to hit that pitch.

Although a batter's average will not be increased if she runs everything out, her percentage of getting on base will rise. A ground ball sometimes can appear so easy that the fielder approaches nonchalantly and errors can result. Whether runs are earned or unearned, they all count the same. It is one thing for a batter to be completely fooled by a good pitch and forced to hit a little dribbler toward third;

it is another thing when the batter fails to run that dribbler out, watches the third baseman have difficulty finding a handle, and knows that had she run the ball out she would have been safe at first. Every time an offensive player reaches base safely, more pressure is placed on the defensive team. Although it feels more satisfying to get on base via a base hit than an error, it also feels better to stand safely on first than to become just another out. Also, the more players who reach base safely, the more runs will be scored.

When batters have passed the stage of simply getting up at bat and trying to hit the ball, different situations can be approached. If a long-ball hitter is at bat with a runner on third base and less than two outs, she must realize that if she cannot get a base hit and hits a long fly ball, the runner on third can still score. The base hit would be nice, but knowing that there is another viable option eases the pressure on that batter.

With a runner on second base, if the batter can hit behind the runner—that is, hit toward right field—that baserunner is almost assured third and has a good chance to score. On a ball hit in front of the runner—that is, toward left field—the runner would have to hold to see if the ball was actually going to go through before she could attempt to head for third.

If a batter has good bat control, run and hit plays are possible. In such an instance, the baserunner leaves with the pitch, enabling her to steal one base and then take the next base on the hit. The key to this play is good bat control and not power, since a ground ball is more valuable than a fly ball, which will be caught.

With a team that likes to steal bases, the batter can assist the runner in her attempted steal by taking a slightly delayed swing and thus miss the pitch. The intentional swing and miss at the ball will distract the catcher enough to provide the runner another fraction of a second longer before the throw heads for the base she wants. Again, bat control is important because if the batter touches the ball she may foul it and force the runner to return to her original base, or, worse, she may pop the pitch up and cause a double play. The batter must also have confidence in her ability to hit, since by taking the intentional strike she will have only two additional strikes left.

BATTING DRILLS

Drill #1. The use of batting tees is particularly helpful in aiding a beginning batter since the ball is stationary and no pitchers are required. Players can work in twos, one using the batting tee and the other fielding the ball. If a chain-link fence is available outdoors, or netting or a padded wall is available indoors, a batter can work by herself, hitting the ball into the fence, net, or wall, which will absorb the impact and permit her to easily retrieve the ball and bat again. This setup also makes it easier for the coach to help since the problem of poor pitches is eliminated.

Drill #2. If mirrors are available, a batter can take practice swings with a weighted bat. The mirrors enable the batter to watch her own swing without doing anything that would injure the development of a good swing. If the batter has her chin tucked into her forward shoulder, she can observe her own swing in the same manner in which she would watch the pitch. Corrections made by the coach in this setting are particularly effective because the batter can actually see herself make the error and see the correction.

Drill #3. For batting practice indoors without using a batting tee, a player stands about 5 or 6 feet to the bat side of the batter and tosses the ball underhand, parallel to some netting. The batter steps toward the netting and hits the ball into it.

Drill #4. A batting machine is excellent because the machine pitches the ball with a minimum of time wasted and does not tire or lose control. The batter stands in front of a batting cage, one player feeds the machine, and the others are in the field to catch the batted balls. Indoors, if the area is large enough, the batting machine should be used with soft softballs instead of regular balls. The soft softballs will not go as far when hit, nor will they rebound as hard off the walls.

Drill #5. Have players take turns fungo hitting to teammates. Although the ball is not pitched to the batter, she will be able to practice her swing. Because of the number of balls hit, she can also begin to build some upper body strength. Batters and fielders can rotate positions every fifty or so hits.

BUNTING

Bunting is an offensive technique whereby the batter more or less permits the ball to hit the bat rather than actually hit the ball with the bat. As in regular batting, the bunt is used to get on base, score runs, and advance runners. When played against a team with a slow infield or a poor fielding pitcher, the bunt can cause considerable confusion and frustration for the defensive team. When playing against a team whose infielders lay back, it is almost impossible for the offensive team to hit a ground ball through for a base hit. However, if the offensive team demonstrates that it is capable of bunting, the defensive team will have to move several steps in to defend against a possible bunt, thus making it also possible for some ground balls to go through the infield. Combinations such as run and bunt make it possible for a runner on first base to reach third on a bunt by the succeeding batter. Depending upon the skill of the batters and baserunners, the bunt has the capability of making the game more exciting for both players and spectators.

The grip on the bat employed in bunting differs from that in regular batting. Although the bottom hand remains

2 or 3 inches from the rounded knob, the upper hand slides up the bat to the point where the barrel widens. The fingers of the upper hand are folded in, with the top of the index finger forming a platform for the bat to rest upon. The thumb of the upper hand extends diagonally up behind the bat, permitting the barrel of the bat to be grasped between the side of the curled index finger and the thumb. It is important that the fingers of the upper hand are not wrapped around the barrel of the bat because the fingers could be caught between the ball and the bat.

There are two types of stances that can be used when bunting—the square-off and the pivot. Both begin with the batter assuming a regular batting stance. In the basic square-off bunting stance, the batter brings her rear foot up parallel to her front foot, the feet about shoulder width apart. This step turns her body so that the batter now squarely faces the pitcher. The square-off stance enables the

Grip for bunting. *The hands are apart; the upper hand is folded into a fist; and the bat rests on the folded index finger, supported from behind by the thumb.*

The pivot stance for bunting. *The batter pivots on the balls of her feet to turn and face the pitcher.*

The square-off stance for bunting. *The batter steps forward with the rear (or right) foot to face the pitcher; the bat is held at the top of the strike zone.*

batter to meet the pitched ball in front of the plate. The bunted ball will then land on dirt rather than on the plate itself, and thus bounce or roll on the dirt. A bunted ball that hits the plate could be directed into foul ground or take a high bounce off the harder surface, thus making it easier for the defensive team to field. Beginning players sometimes have difficulty with this stance since they tend to step out of the batter's box when they move the rear foot up. A variation of the basic square-off stance is to have the batter step back with the forward foot. This eliminates the problem of stepping out of the batter's box but may cause some batters to bunt the ball over the plate rather than in front of the plate.

In the pivot stance, the batter does not step with either foot but merely pivots on the balls of the feet, to permit the shoulders and hips to face the pitcher. With this stance the batter does not have to worry about stepping out of the batter's box and is also able to meet the ball in front of the plate.

Regardless of the stance employed, the batter extends the bat forward, with the arms relaxed and partially flexed at the elbows. The bat is held parallel to the ground at the same height as the top of the strike zone. This aids the batter in resisting high pitches out of the strike zone and in keeping the bat from getting under the pitch and thus popping it up. To meet lower pitches, the bat is lowered not by arm action alone but by flexing the knees to lower the entire body. The bat is not swung forward into the ball, but rather is used to block the path of the ball. Slight downward action of the wrists may also aid in directing the ball downward. The direction in which the bat faces upon contact determines the direction of the bunted ball. Against a fastball pitcher the batter may "give" slightly with her arms to absorb the contact and cushion the rebound of the ball off the bat.

Bunting may be broken down into three classifications: the sacrifice bunt, the bunt for a base hit, and the squeeze bunt. In the sacrifice bunt, as the name implies, the batter gives herself up to advance the baserunner. There is no element of surprise since the batter assumes a bunting stance before the pitch is released. Once notified that a bunt is coming, the pressure is placed on the defensive team fielders and pitcher to handle the play. This situation arises when a team is working to build a tying or go-ahead run with a runner on base and one or no outs. With a runner on first, a sacrifice bunt may be called to reduce the possibility of the next batter hitting into a double play while still advancing the baserunner into scoring position.

When bunting for a base hit, surprise is a vital element. Good placement of the bunt and the speed of the runner are also important. When an accomplished bunter sees the opposing first baseman playing in front of the base or the third baseman playing deep, thoughts of a bunt toward third should take form. When bunting for a base hit, the batter does not assume a bunting stance until the pitch is on its way.

One of the most common forms of the bunt for a base hit is the drag bunt. The drag bunt is executed by a left-handed batter batting from the right side of the plate. Instead of remaining in a bunting stance until the ball contacts the bat, the batter takes a step forward with the rear foot while still holding the bat parallel to the ground. Thus, her body is in motion as the ball is contacted, and she carries or drags the ball with her toward first.

The push bunt has two variations. The first is similar to the drag bunt when executed by a right-handed batter batting from the left side of the plate. In this case, the bunt is pushed toward first base as the batter takes her initial step toward first with her rear foot. The second variation is used against infielders who charge in for bunts. In this instance, the bat is pushed into the ball by a slight extension of the elbows. If well placed, this push will cause the bunted ball to bounce between and past the fast-charging infielders.

The slap bunt or hit begins with the batter taking a bunting stance as the pitcher gets ready to pitch. The lower hand is 3 or 4 inches up from the end of the bat; the upper hand is near the wide part of the barrel. Then, as the pitch is released, the batter rotates her hips and shoulders backward toward the backstop, simultaneously bringing the bat back for a short backswing (hands approximately in front of the rear shoulder) and transferring her weight onto the rear foot. As the bat is brought back, the top hand slides down to meet the bottom hand in a choke grip. The batter may take a short step into the ball along with the short swing of the bat, or she may just shift her weight without moving her feet as she swings. The batter must concentrate to avoid taking a regular backswing and to avoid a long grip on the bat since bat control, not power, is the important element. The fake bunting stance assumed before the delivery of the pitch should start the defensive team in motion, leaving the normal shortstop and second base fielding positions open for a ground ball to go through.

The squeeze bunt may be called for in a late inning when the tying or winning run is on third base. The runner on third should not be in a force situation, and the batter

The slap bunt or hit. *The bat is only brought partway back, to near the rear shoulder; the top hand slides down to meet the bottom hand.*

should possess good bat control. This play also has two versions—the suicide squeeze and the safety squeeze. With the suicide squeeze play, the batter must bunt a particular pitch, regardless of where it is, because the runner from third leaves with the pitch and digs for home. If the batter misses the pitch, the runner is "dead" since the catcher will be waiting with the ball to make the tag. In the safety squeeze, usually the hitter bunts the first strike pitch. The baserunner takes her lead with each pitch, and when she sees the batter bunt the ball, she continues in, digging hard for home.

The following are some general considerations for the batter when bunting. First, she should try not to be over-anxious and should wait for a strike pitch. She must follow that pitch all the way in, until the ball hits her bat. Should she decide that the pitch is too high (high or rising pitches are the most difficult to bunt), she should pull her bat back close to her body and clearly out of the strike zone. The bunter should slightly flex her knees and hips, keeping her weight on the balls of her feet, in order to be able to get away from inside pitches.

Knowledge of the pitch of the field—does it slant toward foul ground or in toward fair ground—is helpful.

This information will help to determine where to place the bunt. If the field slants toward foul ground, the bunt must be angled in toward fair ground.

Knowing how the defensive team reacts to bunt situations is also helpful. Does the third baseman charge all the way in or does she come part-way and then react to the bunted ball? If the third baseman charges all the way in, the batter may want to push the bunted ball past her. Basically, when bunting, the batter's first obligation is to make sure that the ball goes down on the ground because a pop-up could lead to an easy double play.

BUNTING DRILLS

Drill #1. Two players, one with a bat and the other with a ball and glove, face each other, about 6 to 8 feet apart. The player with the bat assumes a bunting stance and the player with the ball gives her an underhand toss. The ball is bunted and fielded alternately, until the bunter has had about twenty-five chances to bunt. The players then switch positions.

Drill #2. Push or drag bunt drill. The positions of pitcher, catcher, first and second basemen are set up on a field. There can be two or more batters taking turns. The pitched ball is bunted toward first four times; on the fifth bunt the batter attempts to beat the throw by the pitcher or first baseman to the second baseman covering first. Then the next batter bunts five times.

Drill #3. The regular infield is set up, and one runner is on first base. The batter must bunt the first pitch toward third as the runner tries to steal second on the pitch and go to third on the bunt. The coach at third will tell the runner to go or stay at second, depending upon the play made on the bunt. For a variation, place the runner on second. This time the runner steals third on the pitch and tries to go home on the bunt.

Drill #4. Squeeze play drill. The infield positions, except second base, are set up with a runner on third base. On the coach's signal, the batter bunts the ball and the runner on third takes a lead in foul ground. Depending upon the coach's signal, the suicide or safety squeeze is executed by the batter. Several players may alternate bunting and running from third.

4

Base Running

One of the most exciting aspects of softball is base running. With good technique, a batter-baserunner may be safe at first rather than out or may pull safely into third base rather than settling for second. Speed is certainly an asset in base running, but good technique is perhaps more important since not every batter-baserunner will possess great speed. With good technique, the average runner can be a good baserunner and the speed demon can become an excellent baserunner.

There are some techniques that apply to base running in general. Running the bases basically involves sprinting— running on the balls of the feet with the arms pumping vigorously rather than running with a slower heel and toe technique. When the batter hits the ball, she will see whether it is a ground ball to the infield or a fly ball to the outfield, instantly evaluate the situation, and plan to run accordingly. Then the most important target becomes the base rather than the ball. Following the ball with the eyes will only serve to slow down the runner. The coaches on first and third have a good view of the play being made, or not made, on the batted ball and can assist the runners with verbal and hand signals. A runner heading for first, hearing her coach repeatedly call "Come on," knows she has to dig a little harder because the play will be close. A runner nearing second who hears her third base coach call "Hit it" or "down," and perhaps catches a glimpse of the coach's arms waving in a downward manner, knows she should slide. By listening to the coach, the runner can concentrate more on the task of running the bases and does not have to watch to see if the right fielder missed the ball or made the play. The harder the runner runs, the closer the play. The closer the play, the more pressure on the defensive team and the more chance of errors due to rushing a play or taking the eyes off the ball to glance at the runner. With the exception of first base, if a baserunner overruns a base she is liable to be tagged out. By listening to and watching coaches' signals, the runner can better prepare to stop at a particular base if necessary.

Whether running to first or tagging bases on an extra-base hit, the runner should always tag the base without altering her running stride. Changing the size of her stride to tag the base with a specific foot or jumping at a base wastes precious seconds.

RUNNING OUT A SINGLE

When the batter hits a ground ball toward an infielder, she automatically knows that she must run as fast and hard as she can to beat that ball to first base. As the batter finishes her swing, she transfers her weight toward her rear foot, thus making it easier to use the rear foot for the push-off and have the forward foot take the initial step. As she runs, her body should lean slightly forward into the run and her elbows should vigorously pump backward and forward. A right-handed batter must cross in front of home plate and head for the outside of the foul line as soon as possible. A left-handed batter has the advantage of starting closer to first base and being already in line with the outside of the foul line. In either case, the batter-baserunner runs as hard as possible in foul ground, until she reaches the base. Then, without breaking her stride, she should tag first base with either foot. Once she has tagged first base, she may slow down as she trails off farther to her right, deeper into foul ground. The running in foul ground is most important on bunted or slow ground balls hit up the first base line. Should a batted ball hit a baserunner in fair ground, the ball is dead and that baserunner is out. Should the baserunner turn toward second base, rather than into foul ground, in order to return to first base after successfully running out a single, her action could be construed as an attempt to try for second and thus she is liable to be tagged out.

RUNNING AN EXTRA-BASE HIT

When a batter sees the ball heading toward an alley between two outfielders or up either foul line, she should start to think "extra-base hit." The batter-baserunner leaves the batter's box in the same manner as she would for a single. Then, about 10 feet before reaching first base, she quickly cuts to the right, into foul ground, and runs in a small arc. This sharp small arc permits the runner to turn, tag the inside corner of first base, and head directly toward second. (Failure to execute a good cut means that the runner will be heading toward second base via right field, again wasting valuable time.) About halfway to second, the baserunner should pick up the third base coach's signals as to whether she should continue to third or stop at second and whether to slide or stand up.

TAKING A LEAD

In softball a baserunner may not leave the base until the ball has left the pitcher's hand. Therefore, as the pitcher gets set, the baserunner, with her shoulders squarely facing the next base, places the ball of her left foot on the ground and pushes her instep against the front of the base. Her right foot is behind the base or farthest from the base she is facing (on first base, the right foot is in foul ground). The runner's knees and hips are flexed, and her head is turned so that her eyes can follow the pitcher's motion. As the pitcher brings the ball back, the runner's weight should be on the rear foot. When the pitcher's arm comes down and forward, the runner's weight should shift over the forward foot; this allows the right foot to take the initial step toward the next base while the left foot pushes off. In this manner, the baserunner's body is in motion while it is still in contact with the base. As the baserunner learns to time the pitcher's motion, her forward momentum begins with the down and forward move of the pitcher's arm, and she leaves the base as the ball leaves the pitcher's hand.

When the steal signal is on, the baserunner continues, running hard, to the next base. If the lead is intended only to provide the runner with the most advantageous position should the catcher miss the ball or the batter hit the ball, the baserunner will stop after several steps. How many steps she takes depends upon several criteria, such as the strength and accuracy of the catcher's arm, whether or not the fielders cover their bases, or if the pitcher lacks control. If the defensive team is alert, a general rule of thumb on steps taken might be the approximate height of the baserunner. A baserunner who takes a lead slightly farther than she is tall should be able to dive back to the base safely.

If the runner takes her lead from second and a ground ball is hit in front of her, to either the shortstop or third baseman, she must stop and be ready to return quickly to second base. That runner on second is of great value to the offensive team since she is in scoring position. But she is

Ready position for a base-runner. *The ball of the left foot is on the ground while the instep and heel are on the base; the right foot is to the side and behind the base; eyes are focused on the pitcher.*

Taking off from the base. *The first step is taken with the right foot while the left foot is still in contact with the base.*

also vulnerable when ground balls are hit in front of her. If the runner does not think and runs forward blindly, she may easily run directly into a tag, perhaps taking away from her team the opportunity for a big inning. However, if she stops and waits until the fielder has committed herself to throw to first, she may be able to advance to third safely on that throw.

All runners when taking a lead from third base should be sure to do so in foul ground. Since many balls are hit down the third base line, a runner at third must be alert to avoid the possibility of being hit by a batted ball. Although taking a lead in foul ground does not ensure that a runner will not be hit by a batted ball, it does ensure that if she is hit, she will not be called out, since the ball is foul. If the runner were to be hit by a batted ball while in fair territory, she would be called out.

TAGGING UP

Every baserunner should automatically take a lead with each pitch. If there are fewer than two outs and a fly ball is hit, every baserunner should quickly return to the base from which she took her lead. The quick return to base will afford the baserunner the opportunity to attempt to advance to the next base after the fly ball is caught. The baserunner may begin her advance as soon as the fielder touches the ball rather than wait until the fielder has firm possession.

If there are two outs, the baserunners do not tag up but continue running with the pitch, since a caught fly ball would be the third out. However, if the baserunners are running and the potential third out is dropped, they have everything to gain because the ball is still in play.

SLIDING

There are three basic types of slides—the straight-in, the hook, and the head first. The straight-in slide is perhaps the safest for beginners. All three, however, have the same purpose—to help the baserunner avoid the tag. When a runner slides, the baseman has to tag only a foot or a hand and not necessarily a player's body. One of the most important things to remember when sliding, regardless of the method employed, is not to hesitate or change one's mind. Among players who have been injured while sliding, the most common comments are: "I wasn't going to slide but I changed my mind" and "I didn't know if I should slide and I hesitated."

To slide or not to slide is basically a baserunner's decision, but an alert coaching staff can help, particularly when the play is initiated from behind the baserunner. For a runner nearing second who sees the third base coach waving her arms in windmill fashion and/or hears the coach call "Come on" or "Keep coming," the decision is simple—just keep running. If the coach has her arms extended upward and forward, palms toward second, or if her arms are extended in front with the fingers pointing toward second and she calls "Stay," the runner knows to slow down and stop at that base and no slide is necessary. Should the coach use a downward motion with her hands and call out "Down" or "Hit it," the runner knows that it is imperative to slide. The same holds true for a runner going to third. For a runner going home, the on-deck batter, by assuming a position on the first base side of home plate, about 10 feet away from the plate, will assist the runner in the decision to slide or not to slide.

How soon a runner should begin her slide depends on her running speed. If she slows down as she begins her slide, she will slide a shorter distance than if she maintains her running speed. By practicing sliding into a movable base, the runner can judge the amount of space required for her slide. A player's size also affects her reach.

The Straight-In Slide

The runner, heading directly for the base, maintains her speed rather than slowing down when she decides to slide. She allows her arms to swing upward and slightly back as she throws her weight backward. This arm motion will prevent the runner from landing on her hands, and perhaps injuring her wrist or arms, as well as help to keep her upper body low and away from the tag. Her take-off leg is bent back under her, while the other leg is extended and raised slightly to avoid touching the ground and catching the spikes or cleats. The actual slide takes place on the rear upper portion of the bent or underneath leg and on the buttocks. The toe of the extended or upper leg contacts the base. The take-off may utilize either foot, whichever is more comfortable or natural for the runner. Although the runner's arms are thrown upward, she should keep her chin tucked in and avoid throwing her head back.

The straight-in slide. *The runner begins her slide approximately a body length from the base.*

The runner makes contact with the ground and slides on the thigh and buttock of her bottom leg; the arms are up and will continue back with the upper body.

The hook slide. *The toes of the runner's upper foot catch the corner of the base.*

The Hook Slide

The hook slide is so named because the toes of the upper leg hook onto a corner of the base while the rest of the body is off to one side. The corner of the base chosen is the one away from the anticipated play. If the player is sliding to the right of the base, the sliding action occurs on the upper rear area of the right leg and buttocks while the left foot contacts the base. If a player slides to the left of a base, the reverse occurs. Whether sliding to the right or left, the weight goes back but the legs are apart, in a semi-stride or scissor position. Care should be taken that the feet are raised high enough to avoid catching the spikes or cleats on the ground. Generally, this is an advanced form of the slide.

The Head First Slide

In the head first slide, the base is tagged by a hand while the rest of the body is slightly to one side. The advantage of going more to one side or the other of the base is to protect

The head first slide. *The slide is started more than a body length from the base; the head is up and the arms are starting to reach forward toward the base.*

The slide finishes as the runner's hand touches the base, with her body to the side.

the head and face from ramming into the glove or base. As the runner approaches the base, she gives a vigorous push with one or both legs and swings her extended arms forward toward the base. The runner's head should be kept up, preventing the chin or face from touching the ground. Keeping the head up, combined with the vigorous thrust of the legs, causes the back to arch slightly so that the landing and subsequent slide occur mainly on the abdominal area and upper thighs rather than on the hands, chest, or knees.

Should a base be dislodged by a runner sliding into it, the baserunner does not have to follow the base. If the baserunner makes no attempt to advance, she is entitled to safely return to the base once it is replaced in its proper position.

BASE RUNNING DRILLS

Drill #1. A batter takes a game-like swing, drops the bat, and runs to first. The coach, standing near first in foul ground, observes to see if the batter moves into foul ground quickly and runs the distance to first base in foul ground. The coach also looks for any changes in the runner's stride as she tags first base. Each batter in turn takes a swing and runs to first. Once the basic technique is mastered, the coach can use a stopwatch to time the runners.

Drill #2. Runners, one at a time, take a game-like swing, drop the bat, and run toward first. As the runner approaches a cone set about 10 feet from first, she cuts out to the right and turns sharply toward second, tagging the

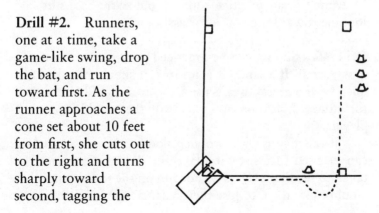

inside of first base. Cones are also placed just outside the baseline, from first to second, to prevent the baserunner from swinging out to right field. The coach observes each runner to see that she does not break her stride while cutting out or tagging first base.

Drill #3. Each runner gets up at the plate, takes a game-like swing, and runs toward first. As the batter begins to run, the coach, near first, calls either a single or extra-base hit. If she calls a single, the runner runs it out and must return correctly to first. The next batter takes her place at home and swings. Again the coach calls either a single or extra-base hit. If the call is extra-base, the runner or runners must look to the coach near third for instructions as to where to run.

Drill #4. One coach fungo hits ground balls. A batter, standing behind and to the right of home plate, runs the hit out. If she is safe, the runner remains on first. The coach again hits a grounder, the runner on first tries for second, and the new batter tries for first. As players are thrown out, they go to the end of the batter line. For variation, a runner may be placed on second, and the coach may vary hitting balls in front of the baserunner as well as behind her. In this way the baserunner will have to decide when to try to advance and when to stay put. If outfielders are added, baserunners can practice running out extra-base hits and looking toward the coach for assistance.

Drill #5. Sliding can be practiced in sand pits or on soft grassy areas. If a sand pit is utilized, it should be raked frequently. If a grassy area is used, the area should be checked for stones, holes, or other hazards that could injure the players.

If practice is on a wooden floor or on grass, a towel can be used to assist the player in sliding. Care must be taken to see that players do not run on the towel, since that would cause them to lose their balance and fall rather than slide. Water can be used to soften a dirt surface to make a "sliding pond" for practice.

Regardless of the practice surface, all players should wear a pair of heavy flannel sweat pants or old baseball or softball uniform pants for protection against burns or scrapes. Players should also remove their spikes or cleats to prevent the danger of such footwear catching on the sliding surface, especially if they are not clear of the ground during the slide.

In landing during a slide, the player should fold one leg underneath while extending the top leg and sit, with the shoulders leaning back and arms up. The coach should check to see that the runner's weight is on the upper thigh of the bent leg and the buttocks. Once a player has the concept of how to safely land, she can take a one- or two-step approach and then go into a slide. The next step would be to approach using a slow jog, then go into the slide. The player should begin her slide 8 or 10 feet from the base. As the player increases her take-off speed, her slide will cover a longer area.

5

The Pitcher

The pitcher holds the key to the success potential of the team more than any other single player, particularly in fast pitch softball. Her ability to consistently throw the ball into the strike zone to force the opponents to attempt to hit the ball is vital to the team effort. No matter how highly skilled the fielders are, unless they have the opportunity to handle ground balls and fly balls, and thus attempt to put runners out, they are helpless.

Pitching takes a great deal of concentration, dedication, and determination. Very few, if any, softball pitchers picked up a ball, decided to become a pitcher, and merely stepped out on the diamond and pitched a game. In most instances, before the pitcher takes the mound for a game she has spent many hours practicing throwing the ball as fast as possible, developing a smooth delivery, and developing enough control to avoid walking or hitting batters. The ability to concentrate fully on the situation at hand is necessary. The pitcher must also be able to maintain her poise in difficult situations. With the winning or tying run on third, she not only cannot afford to throw a wild pitch but must also pitch to the batter in such a way that the batter will not be able to advance that all-important baserunner.

Size and strength are also important attributes of a pitcher. Strong leg and back muscles complement a strong arm. Strength and endurance become particularly important factors in the later innings and in extra-inning games. A longer arm also provides more leverage.

The potential pitcher must also feel a keen interest in pitching. She must be willing to jog several miles a day to build endurance and take time to run sprints and work with weights to increase the strength of those important leg muscles. Of course, pitching itself also helps to strengthen those muscles. The better the pitcher's condition, the longer she will be able to throw effectively.

PRESENTATION OF THE BALL

Regardless of the individual style developed, all pitchers must present the ball before beginning their wind-up. When presenting the ball, the pitcher must have both feet in contact with the ground and the pitcher's plate. Her shoulders must be in line with first and third, and she must hold the ball in both hands in front of her body. The presentation of the ball can take anywhere from 1 to 20 seconds.

In the presentation of the ball, the feet should be approximately shoulder-width apart. For a right-handed pitcher, the right foot is forward and the left foot is back. The forward foot should be placed so that the ball of the foot is on the ground and the rear of the ball of the foot rests against the forward edge of the pitcher's plate. The instep and heel of the forward foot are actually on top of the pitcher's plate. The rear foot is mostly on the ground behind the plate with the toes on the pitching plate. If the pitcher is wearing baseball spikes, the two rear spikes of the

Presenting the ball. *The pitcher has both hands in contact with the ball; her feet are approximately shoulder width apart and in contact with the pitcher's plate.*

forward foot can be placed on the ground in front of and against the pitcher's plate, giving her a more solid area to push off from. Many experienced pitchers dig a hole in which they place their forward foot for the presentation of the ball. In this way the ball of the foot is pushing against the front edge of the pitcher's plate, providing a larger contact area for the push-off foot. Placing the feet so that they contact the front and rear edges of the pitcher's plate also assists in keeping the shoulders parallel to the front edge of home plate and in line with first and third. The ball is held inside the glove with the pitching hand. For the presentation of the ball, the hands are held together, about waist or hip height, in front of the body.

THE BASIC GRIP

Softball pitching utilizes an underhand delivery. The pitch begins when the gloved hand moves away from the ball and the ball starts its downward motion in the pitching hand. The ball is gripped in a similar manner to that used in the regular two- or three-finger throwing grip. Because the pitching motion is underhand, the thumb is across the top seam of the ball and the index and middle fingers are across the underneath seam. The ring finger may be flexed and off to the side. The ball is held in the fingers, by the fleshy pads or tips of the first joints, not in the palm.

PITCHING STYLES

Basic Pitching Motion

The basic pitching motion involves little more than a pendulum-type swing. As the pitching hand brings the ball down and back, the hips are rotated to face toward third base and the weight moves over the forward foot (the right foot for a right-handed pitcher). As the arm reaches the height of the backswing, about shoulder height, the wrist is cocked and the body bends slightly forward from the waist. The rear foot (the left foot for a right-handed pitcher) starts its step forward as the arm begins its downward and forward motion. The arm is slightly bent at the elbow on the downswing and the hips start to turn away from third base toward home. The knees are slightly flexed. On the release, the hips should be facing home plate, the weight transferred onto the new forward (left) foot. The wrist snaps vigorously forward in the vicinity of the knee. The arm continues upward and forward and the new rear (right) foot is brought up even with the left foot to provide the pitcher with a good defensive position. Throughout the entire pitch, the eyes remain riveted on the catcher's target.

Slingshot

The slingshot motion begins after the ball has been presented. The pitcher bends forward from the waist, and the ball, held in the pitching hand, begins its downward and

Basic pitching motion. *As the arm swings down and back, the body rotates toward the right; the elbow is slightly flexed, rather than stiff, and the wrist is cocked.*

When the arm is swung down and forward, the ball is released in the area of the knee.

backward swing. As the ball is swung downward, the body rotates toward third base with the weight shifting to the right, or forward, foot (for a right-handed pitcher). To facilitate the body rotation, the right foot may pivot slightly toward third. As the arm swings back and upward to a full extension of the shoulder, the upper body bends slightly sideward as the hips and shoulders face toward third. The arm should be fully extended at the top of the swing but the elbow should not be locked. The wrist should be cocked. Some rotation of the arm is helpful to obtain a maximum reach backward. The right knee should be slightly flexed, rather than straight. As the arm begins its downward swing, the left foot begins its forward step with the knee still slightly flexed. About halfway through the downswing, the elbow flexes slightly and the hips begin their rotation toward the plate. When the left foot lands, the knee is still slightly flexed. As the arm reaches the side of the body on

After the release, the arm continues upward and the rear foot comes forward.

When the follow-through is completed, the pitcher assumes a defensive position.

the downswing, it should be fairly straight. The shoulders lean a little to the side, pushing the hips out of the way so that the arm can come through almost perpendicular to the ground. The ball is released in the area of the knee. On the release, the right hip is swung sharply around with the aid of a good push from the pitcher's plate by the slightly flexed right leg. This powerful hip and leg action assists the arm in gaining the full power-producing potential of the motion.

On the follow-through, the elbow flexes as the arm continues forward and upward, and the weight transfers onto the forward left foot as the hips now face home plate. The rear, or right, foot is then brought up approximately parallel to the left foot to provide the pitcher a good fielding position. Again, both knees are still slightly flexed. Throughout the pitch, the pitcher's head moves very little and the eyes remain focused on the intended target.

The slingshot pitch. *After the ball has been presented, the pitching arm is swung down and backward; the shoulder is extended; the hips rotate toward third; the eyes remain on the target.*

Partway through the downswing, the elbow is slightly flexed and the wrist is still cocked.

Just prior to the release of the ball in the area of the knee, the arm is perpendicular to the ground.

After the release, the arm continues upward and the right foot is brought up to give the pitcher a good fielding position.

Windmill

Once the ball has been presented, the pitcher leans forward from the waist. The pitching arm, sometimes the glove hand also, reaches forward or the pitching arm alone may drop to the side. As the ball moves away from the body, the weight is transferred onto the right, or forward, foot (for a right-handed pitcher). That weight-bearing leg should remain slightly flexed at the knee. As the pitching arm starts on its upward and backward motion, the left leg starts to reach forward. The hips also begin their rotation toward third. The wrist is cocked as the arm reaches upward and backward. There should also be outward rotation of the arm. On the start of the downward swing, the left leg lands on the ground in line with the right foot. The elbow should not be locked on the downswing, but should be slightly bent to facilitate a smoother motion. The hips begin to turn toward home. The release is accomplished with a vigorous snap of the wrist in the vicinity of the knee. On the release, the hips forcefully turn to face toward home plate with the aid of a strong push from the right leg. On the follow-through the weight continues onto the forward left leg, and the arm, bent at the elbow, continues upward to complete the circular motion. As the weight is placed on the left leg, the right leg is brought up alongside of the left to place the pitcher in a good fielding position. On the follow-through, as well as throughout the entire motion, the knees are slightly flexed to absorb the impact. From the time the pitcher presents the ball until the ball reaches the catcher's glove, her eyes should remain focused upon that glove.

The windmill pitch. *The body leans forward from the waist; arms push forward.*

The arm travels upward and backward; the left leg reaches forward.

The arm is perpendicular to the ground just prior to the release.

The arm continues forward after the release of the ball.

The left foot is on the ground; the shoulder is extended but the elbow has a slight bend.

The arm still has a slight bend at the elbow.

The rear foot is brought up to the left or forward foot.

TYPES OF PITCHES

The spin imparted to the ball upon its release by the fingers will determine whether that ball will drop, curve, rise, or move at a very slow speed. Sideward spinning of the ball causes it to curve to the left or right, back spinning causes the ball to rise, downward or forward spinning causes the ball to drop, and little or no spinning gives the ball a floating effect. The amount of spin and the speed of the pitch will affect the degree to which the ball will break. Different pitchers have various means of imparting a particular spin to the ball. The methods described here are some of the most common.

To obtain a better grip, and thus more spin, the ball is held on its seams by the fingertips. Digging the nail of the index finger or of other fingers into the seam also increases the amount of spin imparted to the ball.

The Curve Ball

When the curve ball is thrown by a right-handed pitcher to a right-handed batter, a ball coming toward the inside corner of the plate will break farther in and contact the handle of the bat rather than the wider barrel. If thrown to a left-handed batter, the ball appears to be heading directly for the batter, only to break back over the plate.

In a commonly used curve grip, the thumb is on the top seam and the index and middle fingers are on the bottom seam. The pitcher takes a short step and cocks the wrist on the downswing. On the release, the wrist snaps up with an outward rotation, causing the fingers to push up and sideways and the thumb to push down and sideways. This imparts a sideward spin to the ball. The pitching arm continues up and to the third base side of the pitcher, with the elbow bent.

The Drop

The drop pitch, as the name implies, breaks downward out of the strike zone as it reaches the plate. The drop is a good pitch to throw to make a batter hit a ground ball.

The ball is gripped with the thumb on the top seam and the index and middle finger or index, middle, and ring fingers on the underneath seam. A short step is taken and the wrist is cocked on the downswing. On the release, the thumb lifts off and the ball rips off the fingertips as the wrist is snapped upward. The arm continues up, almost to shoulder height on the follow-through.

The Rise

This pitch breaks upward, causing the batter to swing under the ball and pop it up. One method of throwing this ball uses a grip with three fingers placed on the top seam and the thumb and little finger underneath, to their respective sides. A long step is taken, and on the downswing the arm is rotated so that the palm is up. Leading with the knuckles forward, the wrist is sharply snapped outward and upward on the release, causing the ball to come off the fingertips. Following a low release of the ball, the arm, led by the hand with the fingers pointing up, continues to about head height.

In another type of grip three fingers are placed on the bottom seam with the thumb on top. A long step is taken, and the wrist is cocked on the downswing. Just prior to the release, the fingers point toward third. As the wrist is snapped up and out in a low release, the fingers rotate under the ball and push up while the thumb pushes back and down. The arm continues upward and forward, toward the plate.

The Change-up

Although usually there are slight differences in the speed of various pitches, they are not always sufficient to prevent the batter from successfully timing deliveries. The change-up is a pitch that comes in so slowly that the batter can almost count the stitches on the ball as it goes by. Once the batter has seen this very slow pitch, the other faster pitches become more effective because the possibility that the pitcher will use the change-up remains in the batter's mind. The change-up is only utilized against strong batters.

Instead of the ball being gripped by placing the fingertips on the seams, it is held farther back in the palm with pressure applied by the thumb and the first phalanges of the fingers. The thumb is on top and the fingers are straight and underneath the ball. On the downswing, the wrist is not cocked but rather in line with the arm. The ball is pushed forward as the fingers and thumb lift away from the ball. The arm continues forward toward the plate to about waist height.

FUNDAMENTAL PITCHING STRATEGY

Once a pitcher has developed her style of pitching and is capable of putting the ball where she wants it, when she wants to, she is ready to think seriously about a pitching strategy. No matter how fast a pitcher can throw, if she does exactly the same thing with every pitch her balls will be hit. Mixing up pitches by shooting for various corners of the plate and changing speeds helps to keep the batter off-balance and guessing. To decide what pitch to throw depends upon the particular batter and the situation.

One consideration when deciding on where to pitch is the batter's stance. If she has a closed stance, inside pitches may be most effective; outside pitches will be more effective on a batter with an open stance. Another consideration is the distance of the batter from the plate. For a batter who stands close to the plate, inside pitches are difficult to hit. Outside pitches are hard to handle for a batter who stands away from the plate.

The batter's grip also helps indicate which pitches will be most effective. A batter who uses a choke grip will not be able to reach outside pitches, and a batter with a long grip will hit inside pitches off the handle instead of off the heavier barrel end of the bat.

If the batter stands tall in the batter's box, low pitches

may be more difficult for her to hit. High pitches may cause more problems for the batter who crouches at the plate.

A pitcher who is able to throw drops and risers can utilize the batter's stance effectively. When a batter stands to the rear of the batter's box, the drop is most effective, and the riser is effective if the batter stands toward the front of the box.

If the pitcher suspects that the batter may bunt, she should keep the ball high since it is the most difficult pitch to bunt. When the pitcher recognizes that the batter is a power hitter, she should try to keep away from that power by pitching low and outside.

Occasionally, an intentional walk may be wise strategy. With one out and the winning run on third, a walk to the batter would set up a double play possibility with the succeeding batter. Also, with runners on second and third, a walk to load the bases would set up force plays at all bases. To consider the intentional walk as a viable strategy, the pitcher must have control and confidence in her ability.

In general, it is better for the pitcher to get ahead of the batter. In other words, the pitcher should try to make the first pitch a good strike pitch. If the first pitch misses, the next two pitches should be strikes. Pitching ahead of the batter—that is, pitching more strikes than balls—puts the batter on the defensive and forces her to protect the plate by swinging at pitches near the corners. If the pitcher is behind the batter—that is, she has thrown more balls than strikes—the batter has more of a choice as to which pitches to swing at.

Moving the ball around and changing pitches is also helpful in keeping the batter off-balance. If the first pitch is high and inside, the next may be low and outside, and so on. Throwing an occasional change-up also makes it more difficult for the batter to time the fast ball. Walking the first batter who faces the pitcher in an inning should be avoided if at all possible. Of any walks issued, that to a lead-off hitter seems to be the one that comes back to haunt the pitcher.

SPEED VERSUS CONTROL

To become a successful pitcher, both speed and control are necessary. Speed without control leads to many walks and batters being hit, while control without speed may tend to allow more base hits.

In the controversy of speed versus control there are sound reasons behind each philosophy. However, the most important issue seems to be the time available before the pitcher must step out onto the pitcher's plate to start a game. In many youth leagues, industrial leagues, and even school conferences, teams may have very limited preseason practice. In this case, the pitcher is forced to concentrate more on control, or she will find herself in a very frustrating position with opponents walking around the bases. However, if a team has an adequate pitching staff or if the prospective pitcher begins at the end of one season to prepare for the next, throwing for speed is probably more advantageous for that pitcher's development. Once the pitcher knows what it is like to throw as fast as she possibly can, her technique can be refined to add the necessary control.

RESPONSIBILITIES OF THE PITCHER

Besides pitching the ball, the pitcher is also responsible for backing up throws to home plate and to third base. In both cases, she should be in foul ground, about 15 or 20 feet behind the base and in line with the throw. Occasionally, on balls hit up the first base line, she may also cover first to take the throw from the first baseman.

The pitcher should charge in to field bunted balls and pop-ups in front of the plate. How much she will field depends partly on her own speed and partly on the experience of the first and third basemen. Of course, ground balls in the area of the pitcher's plate are her responsibility. Pop-ups that hit a little behind the pitcher's plate requiring the pitcher to back up are generally better left to the third or second baseman or shortstop, who would be coming in toward the ball.

Before getting into a position to pitch, the pitcher should check to see that her fielders are ready. The pitcher must also be aware of the number of runners on base and see that they return to base before she pitches. Knowing the number of outs is also a must, since it will determine pitching strategy.

Before she goes out to pitch each inning, the pitcher should confer with the scorekeeper to see which batters she will be facing during the upcoming inning. The pitcher may also check with her catcher and/or coach to determine the best pitching strategy.

PITCHING DRILLS

Drill #1. Draw a 17-inch wide (the width of the plate) rectangular target on a wall. The height should be approximately the knee and armpit height of an average-size batter. Another mark, 2 feet wide, should be placed on the floor 40 feet from the wall (the distance from the rear point of home plate to the front of the pitcher's plate). The pitcher practices by herself, throwing the ball against the wall. At first, the entire rectangle is the target. As control increases, the target becomes more refined and the pitcher tries to hit the lower inside corner, and so on.

Drill #2. A pitcher can work on her motion without a ball in front of a full-length mirror. By keeping her eyes focused straight ahead, she can observe her entire motion and make corrections.

Drill #3. To work on developing speed and endurance, the pitcher stands about 20 feet from a wall. There is no target because the major concern in this drill is throwing for speed. She throws the ball as hard as possible, fields the rebound, and then pitches again. The pitcher can work against the wall in sets of about twenty-five pitches.

Drill #4. Pitching to a catcher. Once the pitcher has a basic amount of control, a catcher can move her target, holding the low outside corner until the pitcher can hit it five times. Then the target is moved and held until the pitcher is able to hit that target five times in succession.

Drill #5. The wall affords good practice for the pitcher who is working on her release or follow-through. The pitcher stands about 10 to 15 feet from the wall and works only on that part of her motion that needs improvement. Utilizing the wall rather than another player enables the pitcher to concentrate on the specific task and not worry about control.

6

The Catcher

The ways in which coaches fill the position of catcher are often strange. "If she cannot catch a fly ball, put her behind the plate." Or, "If she does not know the game, stick her behind the plate and then all she has to remember is to return the ball to the pitcher." Although, in a way, you can chuckle at such reasoning, it is sad for the player and the team.

Instead of being left to chance, the position of catcher must be filled only after serious consideration. The catcher is the one player who has the entire field in front of her. She can observe the baserunners and how they take leads. She sees when her teammates are ready to play, if they are tying a shoelace, or if they are still conferring over a possible play. The catcher is in the best position to remind all of the fielders where the possible plays are and the number of outs. Also, the catcher can remind outfielders to move in for weaker hitters or to the side for pull hitters. The catcher is the player who most helps the pitcher, since she sets the target and calls the pitches. In other words, the catcher is similar to a general: she plays a vital role in the deployment and coordination of the team on the field.

A player in this position must know the game thoroughly. She must be able to assess a situation instantly and make such decisions as "cut the ball" and "throw to second." Certainly, she must possess good basic softball skills. Her short throws to the pitcher must be consistently accurate. She must have the ability to throw to any base quickly and accurately. The catcher must be agile enough to block pitches in the dirt as well as snag other pitches that are high or wide. Good condition, strong legs, and endurance are additional qualities necessary for a catcher.

The catcher requires more equipment than just a glove, uniform, and spikes. She must wear a mask to protect her face and a body protector. The mask must be adjusted for the individual catcher to afford her the most protection as well as an unobstructed view of the ball. The body protector must also fit the catcher (see Chapter 9, Equipment) because a body protector that is too large or too loose can result in more problems and injuries than protection. Throwing and catching the ball with this additional equipment definitely requires a player with good coordination, agility, and above average skills. Although not required, a batting helmet or a special catcher's helmet is an additional safety precaution. To avoid the bruises that can result from foul balls and pitches that go into the dirt and must be blocked, the catcher should wear shin guards to protect her knees, shins, and ankles. To enhance their mobility, some catchers give up the full protection afforded by the shin guards and opt for the lighter, smaller, and less cumbersome regular padded knee guards.

RECEIVING THE BALL

When ready to receive the pitch, the catcher assumes a squatting position in the catcher's box behind home plate.

Depending upon the batter's stance, whether opposite the plate or in front of or at the rear of the batter's box, the catcher assumes her position accordingly. For the batter who stands opposite the plate, the catcher's glove may be close to the rear line of the batter's box. If the batter stands far back in the box, the catcher moves back to avoid the danger of being hit by the bat.

When the catcher assumes her squatting position behind the plate, her weight is on the balls of her feet, and she can actually sit on her heels to relax. When the pitcher is ready to pitch, she changes to a low semi-crouch position. In this position, the feet are shoulder-width apart and the knees are at a 90-degree angle. Buttocks are about knee height. To facilitate a fast throw, the left foot should be slightly ahead of the right foot (for a right-handed catcher). The back is rounded and the chin is in close to the chest with the elbows slightly in front of and above the knees. By keeping the chin close to the chest, the lower part of the mask and the upper end of the body protector combine to

The semi-crouch position. *The knees are bent about 90 degrees; buttocks are about knee level; the throwing hand is behind mitt; the mitt is up.*

protect the throat area. When her glove target is set for a low pitch, the catcher's eyes should just look over the top of the glove. Although this position is demanding, it does enable the catcher to react quickly in order to chase foul balls and wild pitches. It also provides the umpire with an unobstructed view of the pitch from the time it leaves the pitcher's hand until it enters the catcher's glove.

The catcher's throwing hand should be kept in a fist behind her glove target to prevent injury from foul balls while still permitting quick access to the caught ball. The hand, still in a fist, may also be held behind the back, but in this position it takes slightly longer to get the ball into the throwing hand and, thus, to get the throw off.

From the semi-crouch position, the catcher should be able to reach any pitch in the strike zone by extending her arm. This is very important with pitches that come in at the top of the strike zone. If the catcher can catch that pitch by merely extending her arm, the umpire still has an unob-

Lining up the body with an inside pitch. The catcher steps to the left with the left foot.

structed view of the pitch and the likelihood of a favorable call is enhanced. If, however, the catcher jumps up for that pitch, the umpire's view may be obstructed and a "ball" call is more likely.

On balls that come in out of the strike zone, this semi-crouch position offers an excellent starting position. With the weight on the balls of the feet and the legs bent to a 90-degree angle, if the ball is high, the catcher is able to jump up to snag it. If the ball is to the side, the weight can be quickly shifted to the far foot, freeing the near foot to step toward the side closest to the pitch. To block balls in the dirt, a push forward with the balls of the feet brings the catcher down on her knees to prevent the ball from rolling under her. Even if the ball is not caught, by keeping the ball in front of her, the catcher still remains in charge of the situation. The catcher should align her body with each ball, whether it is in or out of the strike zone.

SETTING THE TARGET

When setting the target for the pitcher, the catcher should hold the open glove up and steady. The glove should be kept fairly close to the body, in the area of the knees. With the target arm flexed, the glove should not tip the batter's bat, because the batter would be awarded first base. Also, the catcher's hand will be safer since the possibility of it being hit by the swinging bat should be eliminated.

The placement of the target depends upon the pitching strategy. The catcher should adjust her target glove in consideration of the batter's stance or known weaknesses. On days when the pitcher has trouble keeping the ball from going too far inside, the catcher may actually set her target over the center of the plate for an inside pitch or outside the plate for a pitch on the outside corner. If the pitcher is throwing in the dirt, a target set a little higher than normal may be helpful.

THROWING

Throwing from the catching position is unique because, with the presence of the umpire, there is less space for a backswing. The ball is taken by the throwing hand as soon as that hand can slide around the side of the glove. Also, as the ball is caught, the glove can "give" toward the throwing shoulder in anticipation of the throw. With the elbow bent, pointing out and back, and the wrist cocked, the ball is brought back next to the catcher's ear for the start of the throw. At the same time the weight is transferred to the foot on the same side as the throwing hand. The opposite foot takes one step in the direction of the intended throw. This step is long and low, keeping the catcher's body momentum more forward into the throw than up and then forward. With the elbow leading, the forearm and wrist are snapped up and outward in line with the target. Basically, the catcher utilizes an overhand throw.

The throws must be made to the base, not to the fielder moving toward the base. By the time the throw reaches the base, the fielder should be in position to receive it and complete the play. Getting rid of the ball quickly improves the chances of a successful play. The throw itself must have a low trajectory, almost in a line. The catcher's throwing arm must be both strong and accurate.

Throws back to the pitcher, because of the short distance, are often made from the squatting position using body rotation rather than an actual step into the throw. However, if runners are on base, the catcher must always be ready to throw if necessary. In this situation, after receiving the pitch she may take a step with her arm cocked, to warn the baserunner not to run. If the runner, in turn, offers the catcher a challenge by taking a few more steps, the catcher must not be too anxious to throw. Instead of immediately throwing and committing herself, the catcher should take several quick steps directly toward the baserunner in question. This action usually forces the runner to return to the base she left because the catcher's throwing distance is decreased.

After an extra-base hit, where the ball has been thrown home in pursuit of a scoring runner, the catcher may find herself looking at a second runner, perhaps between second and third. Instead of throwing immediately to third to prevent the runner from advancing, or worse, throwing behind the runner to second base, the catcher should hold on to the ball and run directly at the baserunner. Again, this cuts down the throwing distance and forces the runner to commit herself. If the runner remains still, the catcher should continue moving directly at her and attempt the tag.

When attempting to pick off a runner at third or first, the throw must be quick and to the base. The catcher must not be overanxious and throw to the base that the runner has left. If the runner has taken a large lead, a quick throw behind the runner may play into the runner's strategy and open the possibility of the runner advancing to the next base on the throw to the base behind her. On the other hand, if a runner takes a lead of 8 to 10 feet, she may be challenging the catcher to try to pick her off. If the runner is taking only a lead of 5 or 6 feet, and a dive with her arm extended will easily get her safely back to her base, a pick-off attempt would not be called for.

FIELDING

One of the most difficult skills to be mastered by the catcher is to keep her eye on the ball at all times, even when the batter swings at and hits the ball. This skill is vital to the catcher when balls are popped foul. A catcher who blinks her eyes when the batter swings will take longer to locate both pop-ups and bunted balls.

When a ball is bunted or popped up out in front of the plate, the catcher should immediately flip her mask behind her. This is done simply by putting the thumb of the throwing hand under the lower pad of the mask and pushing upward.

If the ball is on the ground and a throw to first base is necessary, the catcher must field the ball and step directly toward first without taking any unnecessary steps. Often, when fielding ground balls in front of the plate, catchers have a tendency to turn a circle before they throw, which makes an accurate throw more difficult because it takes longer to find the intended target. If the catcher charges the ball, knowing which base to throw to, her approach enables her to step directly toward the intended target. If the ball is rolling toward her left, the catcher should rush out slightly toward her left so that she can come behind the ball and field it with her body open toward first, rather than charge straight out and be forced to reach back toward third to field the ball. The latter technique often leads to the unnecessary circle before the throw.

Many bunted balls can best be fielded with the throwing hand. This technique makes it possible to get the throw off faster than if the ball is fielded with the glove. The faster the catcher can field and throw the ball, the better the chance of getting the runner. Occasionally, some balls in front of the plate have a tremendous amount of spin, making a barehand pick-up impossible. In this instance, the glove hand should be used to smother the ball by trapping it between the glove and the ground. Once the spin has completely stopped, pick up the ball and make the throw.

On pop-ups in foul ground, the catcher immediately takes off the mask but holds on to it until she sights the ball. Only after she knows where the ball is does she throw her mask away. If the mask were to be flipped off in the same manner as for a ball in front of the plate, the catcher may inadvertently make the catch more difficult for herself by having to avoid stepping on the mask as she tries to catch the ball.

COVERING HOME PLATE

Depending upon the situation, there are several ways to cover the plate. If the bases are loaded and there is a possible play at home, the catcher plays the plate similar to the way that a first baseman plays first. When the ball is hit, she rushes out in front of the plate and stretches by stepping toward the throw with the foot on the same side as her glove hand. The toe of the other foot should be in contact with the front edge of the plate. Unless the out at home is the third out of the inning, the stretch becomes important because the sooner the play at home is completed, the sooner another play can be initiated. In a bases-loaded situation, where the run must not be permitted to score, a common double play involves the catcher who tags home for the first out and then throws on to first base for the second force out.

There are two basic ways of covering home plate in a tag situation. In the first method, the catcher stands in front of the plate in fair ground about 1 foot up the third base line, leaving the base path free for the runner. The catcher's knees and hips should be slightly flexed and her weight kept on the balls of her feet. Her feet should be at least shoulder-width apart. If she must tag an upright runner, she is in a position to tag her on the side as she goes by just prior to tagging the plate. In this instance, all body contact is avoided since the base path is free and the only contact with the runner is that of the ball in the glove making the tag. If more body contact than expected occurs, the flexion in the knees and hips will enable the catcher to absorb the force of the impact. Should the runner slide, the catcher merely increases her crouching position and tags the runner's feet as she slides by on her way to the plate. Again, the catcher does not have to worry about being hit by the soles of the runner's shoes in case that runner is inexperienced at sliding.

At a level of play where the baserunners will slide on

any possible tag play, the catcher may straddle home plate much the same way as any baseman covers her base in a similar situation. Again, the catcher should be in a crouching position, with her center of gravity low and her weight on the balls of her feet. After catching the ball, the catcher sweeps her glove hand down to let the runner slide into the tag. Immediately after the tag, the catcher should shift her weight onto the outside foot and lift her inside foot back and out of the base path. This move takes the catcher out of the sliding player's path and leaves her facing toward the field, ready to initiate any necessary succeeding play.

BACKING UP

With no runners on base or with a runner on first, if the batter hits a ground ball the catcher should run toward first base. She runs in foul ground, several feet outside of the base path, until she reaches the vicinity of first base. There she lines up with the throw in foul ground, about 10 feet behind first base. Basically, she will back up any throws that get away from the first baseman on the home plate side of first base as well as throws directly over first base. Throws angled toward right field will be backed up by the right fielder. If no play materializes at first base, the catcher must quickly return to the home plate area.

On throws to third base from the left fielder, the catcher may also back up third base by lining up with the throw in foul ground, partway up the third base line. If the catcher backs up third on such a play, either the pitcher or first baseman must come in to cover home just in case something goes wrong with the play at third. In most instances, however, if the catcher fields the overthrow, she is in excellent position to cut into the base line, in possession of the ball and ahead of the runner.

The catcher can also cover third in certain bunt situations. Often, a runner on first will try to go all the way to third on a bunt by the succeeding batter if third base is left uncovered. With the second baseman going to cover first base and the shortstop going to second base, coverage of third is left to either the pitcher or catcher. Since the catcher is more accustomed to making tag plays, she is better suited to cover third; the pitcher or first baseman can continue her forward momentum and be ready to cover home should the need arise. Therefore, with a runner on first and a third baseman who charges in to field bunts, provided that the catcher is not the one who fields the bunt, she should continue her forward momentum and cover third base.

CALLING SIGNALS

Depending upon the level of play, the signals can vary from very simple to more complex series. The catcher not only signals for pitches but can also call pick-off plays.

Simple signals might include holding the glove low

Catcher giving a signal

and inside to mean pitch the ball low and inside. Touching her throwing shoulder can indicate to the fielders that she anticipates an attempted steal and that there will be a pitchout.

As the pitcher develops a variety of pitches, the signals must keep pace so that the catcher will know exactly what to expect. While in her low squat, with her throwing hand held against the inside of her right thigh, the catcher can signal with her fingers. Her glove hand rests on the front edge of her left knee to block the opposition's view of the signals. Signals can consist of one finger extended for a drop, two fingers for a curve, three fingers for a fastball, and all fingers for a change-up. If two signals are given, signal one can indicate the type of pitch, such as a drop or curve, and signal two can indicate either the inside or outside corner. The signals must be shown clearly and slowly in order to ensure accurate communication to all. Many combinations of signals can be devised, but, in general, the simpler the signals, the less confusion and the better the results.

RESPONSIBILITIES OF THE CATCHER

The responsibilities of the catcher are divided into two categories—those to the pitcher and those to the team in general.

The catcher should warm up the pitcher before a game. If she is not able to work with the pitcher for the entire warm-up period, the catcher should at least work with the pitcher for the last ten minutes of the warm-up. By doing so she can help assess which pitches are working and which are not.

Before the game, the catcher should get together with the pitcher and perhaps a coach to determine a general pitching strategy. Prior knowledge of a team's players can be discussed as well as which pitches are working best that day for that pitcher. If line-ups are available, they can discuss a player-by-player strategy.

The catcher must give clear signals and reminders of the number of outs and runners on base. Should the pitcher become upset because of an unfavorable call or a poor pitch, the catcher is the one who usually is responsible for calming her down.

At times it is possible for the catcher to be able to spot a change in the pitcher's release or delivery that is causing a particular problem. The more accustomed to the pitcher the catcher is, the more assistance she can give her.

Since the catcher runs the team defensively, she must remind the fielders to shift for a pull hitter, back up for a power hitter, or come in for a weak hitter. Discussing the opponent's previous time at bat with the scorekeeper before taking her place on the field can help refresh her memory as to which opponent did what.

Calling the play is also an important responsibility of the catcher. When balls are being relayed in from the outfield, it is the catcher, with full view of the entire play, who should initially call where the throw should be made.

Before she proceeds to send signals to the pitcher or put up her glove as a target, the catcher must check to see that all of the fielders are ready. If a fielder is having a problem, or if people are starting to walk across the outfield, the catcher is closest to an umpire for requesting a time out. When the catcher puts up her target, both the pitcher and the fielders should have the confidence that everyone is ready to handle whatever may occur as a result of the next pitch.

CATCHING DRILLS

Drill #1. To help the catcher learn what strike pitches she can reach without having to stand up, a player tosses balls to her from a distance of about 15 feet. The catcher should be wearing her full gear. The same arrangement can be used to help the catcher learn how to block balls in the dirt. The tosser intentionally tosses the balls into the dirt so that the catcher must drop to her knees or step to the side and drop to one knee to block the ball. At first, the balls can be thrown softly; as the catcher becomes accustomed to going down to block balls, the tosses can be harder. This will also help the catcher develop confidence in the protective quality of the equipment she uses.

Drill #2. The coach hits foul pop-ups. The catcher must push her mask up, locate the ball, and then toss the mask away from the play area as she starts to go after the ball.

Drill #3. The ball is bunted by the coach in such a way that the catcher must field it. The catcher rushes out, fields the ball, takes one step, and fires the ball to first base. Add a shortstop and the play can be changed to second base. Baserunners may be added once the players are accustomed to making the play.

Drill #4. With a runner on first base, the coach bunts the ball so that it must be fielded by the charging third baseman. The shortstop covers second and the second baseman covers first. The first play must be made to first. The runner on first tries to reach third before the catcher can get into position at third to take the throw from first base. A runner from home to first may also be added.

Drill #5. The coach hits ground balls to the second baseman, who fields the ball and throws to first base. The catcher runs down in foul ground to back up first base on each hit. Throws are intentionally permitted to go through to give the catcher practice in lining up with them.

Drill #6. Throwing to bases can be practiced by setting up a pitcher, second baseman, and catcher. The pitcher throws the ball to the catcher; then the catcher fires the ball to second. The pitcher gets used to ducking down so that the catcher can see second, and the catcher becomes accustomed to throwing over the pitcher's head.

7

Putting It All Together

OVERALL OFFENSIVE AND DEFENSIVE PLAY

The key to overall offensive and defensive play is the team concept and communication. Each player must develop her own individual throwing, running, catching, and batting skills to the best of her ability. Then, the concept of how the individual player best fits into the overall picture must be understood.

As players come to understand their strengths and weaknesses, a team concept can develop. It becomes the responsibility of the coach to utilize the strengths of each player to the benefit of the entire team. A player who is not a strong batter but possesses an excellent throwing arm and catching ability may share an outfield position with another player who has a high batting average but only an average arm and catching ability. Just as the latter provides offensive punch to help build a lead in the early innings, the former provides the defensive ability to maintain the lead through the final innings. A similar situation, on the offensive side, occurs when a strong hitter leads off the last inning with a double, to put the winning run in scoring position. Then that hitter, who may not be a strong baserunner, may be replaced by a fast knowledgeable runner who will be able to take advantage of her good position to actually score that important run. In this way, each player contributes her strength to the whole team effort.

Another example of utilizing individual player skills is in the development of the line-up. The first third of the batting order combines such skills as a "good eye," speed, bunting, hitting singles, and, in general, getting on base. The middle third of the line-up usually provides the power—the long ball—to send the baserunners home to score. The last third of the line-up may be weaker batters. When the bottom of the order gets on base, the top can move them around by bunting or walking and setting up the bases for the long-ball hitters. A double or triple with no one on base puts only one runner in scoring position, but a base hit with runners on bases scores runs. Many more runs are scored through a total team effort than by relying solely on a home-run hitter.

Perhaps one of the most graphic examples of the whole team concept occurs when players back up one another. Not only do the pitcher and catcher move on every pitch, but so does every player on the field. After every pitch, there is a ball to be fielded and/or a throw to be made. Thus, there are bases to be covered and fielders and throws to be backed up. When the second and third basemen cover their bases with a runner on second, that runner must be careful of her lead and will not be too likely to run. When first and third are backed up, if a throw gets past either baseman, the runner will be held at first or third, minimizing the effect of the error. Thus, the shortstop who made a beautiful backhand play on a ground ball going into the hole between third and short, but whose throw went into the dirt and past the first baseman, will not get uptight and be afraid to throw the next time. True, the runner is safe at first, but had the shortstop not attempted to field the play and the ball had gone through to the outfield, the runner might have been able to reach second on that hit. Because the throw was backed up, no damage was done, and if the play presents itself again, the shortstop will not be afraid to attempt it again. The next time an out may result.

Knowledge of the opposition and utilization of this knowledge require a team effort. This knowledge may be gained from scouting or watching the team play as well as actual experience playing against that team. The scorekeeper who not only records what the opposing batter did but also where she hit contributes to the knowledge bank. Instead of merely sitting on the bench, bemoaning the fact that they are not out on the field, the players on the bench can make a considerable contribution to their team by observing the opposition, perhaps picking up signals or habits of an opposing player that indicate whether she will run or bunt. Knowing that opposing player number 22 is a pull hitter, and setting the defense accordingly, can turn that extra-base hit down the line into a single or even an out. Knowing that with a particular lead-off batter on first base, the second batter will bunt on the first pitch, enabling the runner on first to steal second on the pitch and go to third on the bunt, will help the defensive team devise a strategy to thwart the play (perhaps by going for the play at third). If outfielders check with the scorer as to who will be batting for the opposition in the next inning, they can gauge how deep to play. With the bottom of the order coming to bat, they can play a little shallow as compared to backing up when the heart of the order comes to bat. By doing this, fewer short fly balls will drop in for base hits and fewer long fly balls will go over the outfielders' heads. In general, building knowledge of the opposition helps a team to utilize its strengths and abilities to its best advantage. In this sense, putting it all together involves all of the team members, those on the bench as well as those on the field, the coaches, and the scorekeepers.

The second major factor involved in putting together

the overall offensive and defensive play is communication. Basically, communication has two forms: verbal communication and communication through signals.

Simple communication, such as a shortstop telling her second baseman that she will cover second on an attempted steal, makes the difference between a possible out and a ball sailing into center field because each thought the other was going to take the throw. A team may have the catcher with the best arm in the league and an excellent shortstop and second baseman, but unless each knows what the others are going to do, all of that skill and ability is wasted. On the offensive side, a team may practice running techniques by having the runner on first steal second and go to third on a bunt. In practice, the coach tells the players what to practice and everyone knows what is going to be attempted. In a game situation, if the coach calls out to the players and tells them what to do, not only will her players know what is expected, but so will the defensive team. Therefore, through the use of signals the coach will tell the batter to bunt on a certain pitch, and then inform the baserunner so that she is prepared to carry out her part of the play. Players must be alerted to what is expected of them and to possibilities.

Alertness is a key factor in the success of a team. When a team is alert and ready for various possibilities, the number of mental errors declines and the amount of intelligent plays increases. No matter how hard you practice and how great your skill, sooner or later you will commit a physical error. But the effects of these errors can be minimized. The errors that hurt the most are the mental errors. When the batter lays down a sacrifice bunt and the runner forgets to run is an example of a mental error that hurts. When a pitcher strikes out the opposition's leading hitter with two outs and the winning run on third, and the catcher drops the ball and walks off of the field thinking that the game is over instead of picking up the pitched ball and completing the play to record the final out—that hurts. In one situation, the possibility to score is lost; in the second, a game is lost. By communicating, mental errors can be eliminated because communication keeps a team alert.

One of the simplest forms of communication that encourages intelligent play is simply calling and responding to the call of the number of outs and the possible play. A call such as "Two down, any base" alerts each baseman that if she fields a ball close to her base, all she has to do is step on that base to get that last forced out, thereby avoiding a long throw and a possible error. If an outfielder knows that there are two outs with the winning run on third base, she knows that she must attempt to catch that short fly ball before it drops because if she were to play it safely and let it bounce, the winning run would definitely score.

Generally, most players, even those just beginning to learn the game, know that a coach gives signals. In the beginning signals are very simple—a coach touches her hat or shoulder or stands facing the batter or at the upper end of the coaches' box. As the team progresses and the opposition grows more alert, signals become more complicated and sophisticated, and they can be given in a series with a certain number indicating which is the actual signal. Through these means, batters and baserunners are told which skills to utilize and when.

Most players are also aware of the fact that the pitcher pitches to a batter in a way that is controlled by the catcher's signals. Those same signals, relayed by infielders, can also alert the outfielders to what may occur. If a pitcher is going to pitch away from a batter's power—that is, pitch outside to a pull hitter—a clenched fist or an open hand held behind her back by the second baseman may alert the right fielder to expect a possible play.

RELATIONSHIP BETWEEN OFFENSE AND DEFENSE

The offense and the defense complement each other. The offense scores the runs and the defense attempts to keep the opponents from scoring. A strong defense complements a strong offense, but it is a necessity when one has a weak offense.

Even a weak hitting offense can put pressure on the opposing defense if the players are alert and ready to take advantage of the opponents' mental and physical errors. Once a player has reached first base, she can often put herself into scoring position or at least eliminate the possibility of a double play by being alert. If the opposing defense does not back up throws to the pitcher or cover its bases, an alert runner could steal second and thus put herself into scoring position. Or, on a bunt, if third is left uncovered, an alert baserunner could go all the way to third if she took a good lead and was aware of the availability of the base. By taking advantage of the opposing defensive team's weaknesses, even a weak hitting team can build enough runs to reduce the pressure of a low-scoring game on their own defense.

In a similar vein, by being alert to the opponents' offensive capabilities and weaknesses, a defense can help to prevent pressure from being applied. A defensive team that covers bases can often keep opponents from attempting to steal and can thus provide for possible double play situations. With two outs, a defensive team that knows its opponents may have an easier and safer play at second on a slow runner than the usual play at first on the batter-baserunner. By being alert to the situation, a defensive team will attempt the easy force play at first for the third out rather than a tag play on the runner from third, who is not forced. An alert shortstop, who is aware of a large lead by the runner on second, will also be aware of the possibility of playing that lead runner if a ground ball is hit her way. After all, it will take a runner on first base longer to score than one on third. The more runners kept from reaching scoring positions or removed from scoring positions, the fewer runs a defensive team will give up. Therefore, besides a relationship between the offense and defense of one team, there is also a sort of relationship between the offense of one team and the defense of the other. The more pressure one team's offense can place on the opposing team's defense, the more pressure is relieved from the first team's own defense. The more difficult one team's defense makes scoring for the opposition, the less pressure is placed on its own offense.

8

Training and Conditioning

GENERAL AND SPECIFIC CONDITIONING

Conditioning of athletes plays an important role in the success factor of any team in any sport. Athletes with muscle injuries sit on the bench rather than play. Athletes who are not in good physical condition and do not possess the stamina and endurance to put forth their maximum effort for ninety minutes without becoming unduly fatigued are more prone to injury. Since softball is a seven-inning game, athletes who are able to play with intensity for only four innings in the hot sun and/or high temperature often end up on the short side of the score by the end of the game.

Conditioning takes more than a two-week period prior to or at the beginning of spring practice; it is a year-round program. An athlete who changes from one sport to another has a period of adjustment in which the body accommodates to the use of various muscles in differing ways. If the athlete is basically fit—that is, if she possesses a good level of general endurance and her muscles have a basic strength—her period of adjustment is relatively pain-less and short.

Many athletes today, particularly those attending educational institutions that offer interscholastic or inter-collegiate athletic programs, participate in more than one sport. The same is true for many athletes out of school who remain active by engaging in other activities once the soft-ball season is over. Another team sport, such as volleyball, often attracts softball players as individuals and sometimes as entire teams. Depending on the level played and the cor-responding length of the season, there may be little or no overlap. If there is an overlap of seasons, the condition in which the player arrives usually more than compensates for the occasional practice missed. Basketball is another team sport that attracts softball players. Individual sports, such as racketball, karate, cross-country skiing, judo, and jogging, interest still others during the off-season months. There are many other sports that could be included, depending on the area of the country and individual interests. Regardless of the activity chosen, the athlete has the opportunity to main-tain a fairly high degree of muscle fitness, endurance, and mental alertness.

Some coaches recommend off-season fitness mainte-nance programs combining jogging and running with stretching and strengthening exercises. Such programs can be arranged by the athlete to coincide with her other activ-ities and responsibilities. An athlete could jog and run three days a week and exercise the intervening two days. Some athletes may enjoy running against the clock on a local park or school track; others may prefer running along different trails through parks or along city streets. The exercise por-tion of the program may involve using Universal Gym, Nautilus, Cybex, or Mini Gym equipment at a local school or health club or may be merely a series of stretching and strengthening exercises the athlete can do in her own home.

When utilizing an exercise machine such as the Uni-versal Gym, the following question must be raised: What is the correct amount of weight for a beginner to push? Generally, the answer depends upon the number of repetitions an individual can do at a particular weight. If the athlete cannot complete a minimum of six repetitions, lower the amount of weight. If she can accomplish twelve repetitions, increase the weight.

One set of ten to twelve repetitions of each exercise every other day will not be harmful. The every-other-day regimen is important because muscles require a rest period after strength workouts. Jogging or running, however, may be carried out on a daily basis with no ill effects.

Where players do not have access to a Universal Gym, they can improvise their own by utilizing a rubber bicycle inner tube. The size of the inner tube may vary, depending on the height of the individual. The shorter the individual, the smaller the inner tube should be. The following are a few sample exercises against resistance which may be executed utilizing a bicycle inner tube.

1. Stand with the arms bent at a 90-degree angle, with the elbows close to the body and the feet shoulder width apart. Hold the inner tube in the upturned hands, permitting the tube to hang freely in front of the body. Step on the lower end of the inner tube with the feet, keeping them shoulder width apart. With the palms turned up, the wrists and elbows are flexed against the resistance created by the stretching inner tube by pulling the knuckles toward the shoulders. If the hands are held palms down, the wrists may be extended against the resistance by raising the backs of the hands toward the shoulders.

2. Stand behind a strong kitchen chair with one side of your body near the center of the chair back. Place the rubber inner tube on the floor around the four legs of the chair and against the outside of the ankle of the leg furthest from the chair back. Apply pressure against the chair to prevent it from moving by

holding onto it with the closer hand. Raise the outside leg out to the side, away from the other leg and against the resistance supplied by the stretching inner tube. Next, step outside the inner tube with the outside foot, extend the arm holding the chair and permit the inner tube to rest against the inside of the ankle of the leg closest to the chair back. With the weight supported by the outside foot, pull the inside leg toward the middle of and across in front of the body against the resistance supplied by the stretching inner tube. If the tube is too large to provide adequate resistance, wrap it around the front legs of the chair to shorten it and increase the resistance.

3. Sit on the floor and place the inner tube behind and against your back, holding onto both sides with the hands and permitting the larger portion of the tube loop to hang loosely in front. With the legs bent, place the soles of the feet against the loose part of the loop. Roll backward until your back is on the floor and the soles of the feet are facing up. Extend the legs against the resistance of the stretching inner tube. Resistance may be increased by pulling the tube harder with the hands.

WARM-UPS

Although there is an ongoing controversy over the benefits of warm-up activities prior to games in improving performance and preventing injury, such activities are still very acceptable and encouraged. Many teams carry over a shortened version of their spring training exercises into pregame warm-ups. The team can form a circle or other formation as soon as the players arrive, and the captain or other designated player leads a short set of general exercises prior to picking up the gloves, balls, and bats. After the general warm-up, the players usually continue to warm up by throwing and catching in twos, followed by pepper, batting practice, and infield drills.

Generally, warm-ups, whether prior to games or to practice, serve to get the athlete ready for the impending workout. Muscles and ligaments are gradually stretched to help prevent strains, tears, and soreness. Warm-ups also help the athlete attain the mental alertness necessary for play and help develop a sense of teamwork. Warm-up exercises that precede the skill warm-up can last about 10 minutes and may consist of easy running and/or jogging, some gradual stretching, and some general body conditioning exercises. On a cool day or evening, the warm-up period may be slightly longer. A sample pre-game warm-up could include the following:

1. Easy jog around the field
2. Circle stretchies (about 10 repetitions each)
   Back stretch
   Trunk stretch
   Hamstring stretch
   Quadriceps stretch
   Trunk circles
   Gastrocnemius stretch
   Groin stretch
   Shoulder stretch
   Neck Stretch
3. Throwing and catching in twos
4. Pepper in groups of three or four
5. Batting practice
6. Infield/outfield drill

Exercises that are part of a conditioning program are longer in duration and more strenuous in nature than those utilized in pre-game warm-ups. Such conditioning exercises generally take two forms. One is calisthenic-type exercise (stretchies and strengthening) and running; the second involves game-related exercises. Both increase the athletes' endurance and general firmness, but the latter also aids in the development of basic skills, eye-hand coordination, and timing. The following are some sample exercises that may be utilized for warm-ups and in conditioning programs.

STRETCHING EXERCISES

Stretching exercises relax the muscles. A particular muscle group is slowly stretched as far as possible without undue discomfort, that position is held, and then the muscles are slowly allowed to return to the starting position. As the athlete stretches the muscles, she should exhale. She holds her breath during the hold phase and inhales during the return to the starting position. In the beginning, the stretch may be held for 3 seconds, gradually building to 10 seconds. Also, each exercise may be repeated about three times in the beginning, then gradually increasing to 10 or 15 repetitions. Exercises may also be done in two or three sets of 10 or 15 repetitions each.

Back, Hips, and Legs

1. Supine position, arms extended sideways at shoulder level, legs together. The hip is flexed and rotated as one leg is raised and moved across to touch the opposite outstretched hand. After the foot has touched the hand, the leg is returned to the starting position next to the other leg. Then the other leg is stretched toward the other hand. If the foot cannot touch the opposite hand, the individual reaches as far as she can. The knee should be kept straight throughout the exercise.

2. Supine position, arms at sides, palms down, legs extended and together. Legs are raised upward and brought over the head, permitting the toes to touch the floor beyond the head. The head, shoulders, and

toes are in contact with the floor. After holding for several seconds, the legs are raised up and then lowered to the starting position on the floor. Again, if the individual cannot touch the toes to the floor, she extends as far as she comfortably can.

3. Sitting, legs extended diagonally to the sides. Hands slide down one leg, toward the ankle, and grasp the ankle, if possible. The face is pulled toward the leg. The individual returns to the sitting position and then stretches toward the other leg. In a variation, the legs are extended and kept together rather than apart.

4. Standing, feet together. Arms reach down toward the ankles, pulling the head toward the legs. Knees should be kept straight. After the hold, the individual slowly returns to the starting position.

5. Standing, feet apart. Hands reach down to the floor and slide along the floor toward the rear of the body. Hold the stretch, then return to a standing position.

6. Standing, feet crossed so that the outside borders of the feet touch. Knees should be kept straight as the individual reaches down toward the floor with her hands. After the hold, return to a standing position, reverse the feet, and then stretch toward the floor again.

7. Standing, balancing on one foot with the other leg bent at the knee. One hand grasps the toe of the bent leg and pulls it toward the buttocks. After the hold, the leg is extended toward the floor and the exercise is repeated with the other leg. If balance is a problem, one hand may be placed against a wall for balance.

8. Kneeling, toes pointing outward. Sit on the heels and place hands on the floor, palms down, fingers toward the front. Permit the head to reach back and raise the hips as high as possible. Hold, then return to starting position sitting on the heels.

9. Standing, palms against a wall about shoulder height. Keeping the feet flat on the floor and the shoulders, hips, and knees in line, flex the elbows until the forehead touches the wall. Hold, then straighten the arms to return to the starting position. Outdoors, two players may join hands and push against each other.

10. Standing, feet shoulder-width apart. Raise up on toes, hold, and return to regular standing position. Raise the outer borders of the feet off of the floor, hold, return to regular standing position. Raise the inner borders of the feet off the floor, hold, return to regular standing position.

Groin

1. Sitting, knees flexed, soles of feet together and close to the body, hands grasping the ankles, elbows on top of the inside of the knees. Pushing down with the elbows, push the outer surface of the knees toward the floor as the upper body reaches forward. Hold, then return to sitting position.

2. Sitting, legs stretched as far to the sides as possible, hands on the floor in front of the body. Slide the hands forward as the chest reaches toward the floor. Hold and return to a sitting position.

3. Standing, feet wide apart. Turn one foot perpendicular to the other and bend that knee, permitting the body to reach over that knee while keeping the other foot flat on the floor. Hold, return to a standing position, and repeat over the other leg.

Shoulders, Arms, and Trunk

1. Standing, feet together, one arm extended at the side, the other reaching overhead. The trunk is stretched toward the side as the extended arm slides

down the side of the leg and the overhead arm pulls over. Hold, return to standing position, and repeat in opposite direction.

2. Standing, arms extended forward at shoulder level, feet shoulder-width apart. Keeping the feet flat on the floor, rotate the body to one side by reaching around to that side and to the rear with the extended arms. Hold, return to front position, and then repeat to the other side.

3. Standing, feet shoulder-width apart, hands on hips. From the waist, lean forward and then rotate the upper body to one side, to the rear, and to the other side. Repeat in the opposite direction.

4. Standing, feet shoulder-width apart, arms extended sideways at shoulder level. Rotating the arms from the shoulder joint, make small slow circles backward, first gradually increasing the size of the circles and then decreasing their size. Reverse direction and circle forward.

5. Standing, arms extended forward at shoulder level. Extend and flex the fingers.

6. Standing, feet shoulder-width apart, arms extended to the sides at shoulder level, palms up. Reach backward as far as possible with both hands simultaneously. Hold, then return to starting position.

7. Standing, arms relaxed at the sides. Flex neck as far forward as possible, chin toward chest. Extend neck as far as possible, and then return to regular standing position.

8. Standing, arms relaxed and at the sides. Moving the head sideways, try to touch the right ear to the right shoulder. Return the head to an upright position, and then try to touch the left ear to the left shoulder.

9. Standing, feet shoulder-width apart, hands clasped behind the body. Raise arms as high as possible behind the body. Do not bend from the waist, and keep the head up. Return to starting position.

10. Standing, feet shoulder-width apart, hands clasped in front of the body. Without unclasping the hands, turn the hands to a palms down position. Raise arms together over the head and reach as far back as possible. Hold and return to the starting position.

STRENGTHENING EXERCISES

Muscles that are too loose or too weak leave the athlete vulnerable to dislocations and other joint injuries. While stretchies aid in maintaining or increasing flexibility, strengthening exercises help keep or develop the muscles so that the joints may safely go through a full range of motion. Such exercises are an important part of the preseason conditioning program. The following are some examples of general conditioning exercises. The number of repetitions will vary depending on age and general condition. Begin with a number of repetitions that can be accomplished without undue strain, and then gradually increase the number of repetitions to about ten.

1. Wall sit. Sit with the feet flat on the floor, knees at a 90-degree angle, and the back firmly pressed against a wall. The same may be accomplished by having two players sit back to back.

2. Push-ups. Weight is borne on the hands and toes. Heels, knees, hips, and shoulders must be kept in alignment. Slowly flex the arms until the chest touches the floor and then extend the arms until they are straight. Start with about three repetitions and increase to about ten. If the athlete cannot keep her body in alignment from the toes to the shoulders, try push-ups from the knees rather than the toes. When the athlete can accomplish ten short push-ups, she should try the full-length push-up.

3. Bent knee sit-ups. Supine position, knees bent, feet flat on floor. For the beginner, arms may be

extended in front of the body; for the intermediate, folded across the chest; or for the more experienced, hands may be clasped behind the head. A light weight may also be held behind the head for the more fit athlete. Regardless of arm position, the head, then the shoulder, and gradually the back are curled up off the floor so that the head or elbows touch the knees. Then the lower back, upper back, and head gradually uncurl until they are again flat on the floor. The trunk may be twisted on the upward phase so that alternately the opposite elbow and knee touch.

4. Stair or bench step. Step up onto a bench about 1 foot high and then down. Start with about ten repetitions, then change the lead leg.

5. Run in place, raising knees about waist height. Start with about 50 steps, 25 with each leg.

6. Jumping/hopping (with or without ropes). Take 10 jumps on both feet, then 10 on the right foot, and then 10 on the left foot. Repeat 5 times.

7. Standing, feet shoulder-width apart, palms pressing against each other, fingers up, about shoulder height. Press palms against each other for a count of five, then relax. Repeat about 5 times.

8. Standing, feet shoulder-width apart, fingers hooked together in front of the chest. Pull away for a count of five, and then relax. Repeat 5 times.

9. Prone position, arms extended over head, legs together. Raise both arms 3 to 4 inches off the floor and hold for a count of five. Lower arms to the floor and relax. Repeat 5 times.

10. Supine position, knees slightly flexed, arms overhead, holding on to a rod or light weight. Raise arms 3 or 4 inches off the floor and hold for a count of five. Lower arms to the floor and relax. Repeat 5 times.

11. Standing, feet shoulder-width apart, arms with elbows bent in front of body, hands holding a stick

with the knuckles up. (Tie a light weight to a small length of broom handle with a 3-foot cord.) By alternately extending and flexing the wrists, wind the string onto the stick.

12. Standing, feet shoulder-width apart, arms with elbows bent in front of body, hands holding a stick with the palms up. (Tie a light weight to a small length of broom handle with a 3-foot cord.) By alternately flexing and extending the wrists, wind the string onto the stick.

13. Wall pulleys. If wall pulleys are available, they may be utilized for strengthening exercises.

   Overhand throw. Stand with back toward the pulley, elbow of the throwing arm flexed, and hold on to the pulley, opposite foot forward as in the throwing position. Pull the weight forward by extending the elbow and flexing the wrist. Repeat 10 times, then rest.

   Underhand throw. Stand with back toward the pulley, throwing arm extended downward at the side, and hold on to the pulley, opposite foot forward. Pull the weight forward by flexing the elbow and wrist. Repeat 10 times, then relax.

   Legs. Stand sideways to the pulley, with the pulley attached to the ankle farthest from it, opposite arm braced against the wall. Extend or adduct the leg sideways. Repeat 10 times and then turn around and change legs. In a similar way, wall pulleys may be utilized for leg adduction and hip extension.

14. Ankle, body, and wrist weights. Such weights may be worn for part of the conditioning exercise workout to provide some increased resistance to the muscle action. Many such weights consist of a series of pockets that contain individual metal bars. The beginner can start with a few weights and gradually increase the number until all the weights are being used.

15. Hand weights. Exercises involving wrist flexion and extension and arm abduction and extension over the head can include small hand weights to provide increased resistance to aid strength-development exercise.
16. Stand in a doorway, feet shoulder-width apart, arms bent with palms pressed against the sides of the doorway at about shoulder level. Push against the sides of the doorway, hold for a count of five, and then relax. Repeat 10 times.

EXERCISES INVOLVING SOFTBALL TECHNIQUES

1. Two players standing about 6 feet apart start jogging forward (around the gym or infield). One player tosses a ball to her partner, who catches the ball and tosses it back. Both players should be able to progress around the area, throwing and catching a ball, without breaking stride or missing the ball. Other sets of two players start out at about 10-foot intervals, depending upon skill level. Gloves may or may not be used.
2. Players are in a circle formation with two players at opposite points outside the circle. The ball is flipped back and forth across the circle while the two outside players try to tag the player in possession of the ball. If a player is tagged while in possession of the ball, she changes places with the outside player. Outside players work on following the ball and footwork, and the circle players work on handling the ball and keeping track of the taggers. Emphasis may vary. By tossing the ball farthest from the taggers, taggers must run more. By tossing the ball closer to the taggers, the ball handlers must react faster to get rid of the ball faster. As players become more proficient, two balls can be used.
3. Two players face each other in a semi-crouch, about

5 feet apart. Player 1 alternately rolls a softball to the left and to the right of Player 2, who alternately crosses over, fields the ball, and tosses it back to Player 1. Neither player straightens up until after the drill is completed. Both players keep their weight on the balls of their feet, with knees and hips flexed.

4. Same as number 3, except two balls are used. As Player 2 picks up the first ball, Player 1 rolls the second ball in the other direction.

5. All players except Player 1 line up behind one another. Player 1 stands about 15 feet away, facing the line of players. Player 1 rolls the ball toward the first player in the line (Player 2), who runs in, fields the ball, throws it back to Player 1, and continues to run just past her. Player 1 then rolls the ball toward the next player in the line and then runs to the end of the line. Player 3 fields the ball and throws it to Player 2, who has replaced Player 1. Player 3 continues to run forward toward Player 2, who rolls the ball to the next player in the line. The drill continues as players keep rotating.

6. Establish a line on the ground with Player 1 about 10 feet away from the line on one side and Players 2 through 5 about 20 or 30 feet away from the line on the opposite side. Player 1 rolls the ball toward the line. Player 2 runs in and tries to field the ball before it crosses the line. After Player 2 fields the ball, she flips it back to Player 1 and runs to the end of the line. Each player in turn fields the ball. Player 1 begins by rolling the ball slowly, but then gradually increases the speed of the ball, forcing the fielders to run faster as endurance increases.

7. Players in a single file line jog toward first base, turning out around a cone or other marker placed just before first and sprinting toward second. They then jog toward third base, turning out around a cone or other marker just before third and sprinting toward home. Alternate jogging and sprinting may

be continued for a specific number of laps or a specified amount of time.

8. Mark off four lines 10 or 20 feet apart, depending on the space available. Two players stand on opposite sides of line 1. Player 1 tosses the ball in a looping fashion toward line 2. Player 2 runs toward line 2, catches the toss, stops and turns, and throws back to Player 1. Player 2 quickly returns to line 1. Player 1 then tosses the ball toward line 3. Player 2 runs to line 3, catches the ball, stops, returns the throw, and runs back to line 1. Play is repeated with line 4 twice, then in reverse with line 3 and line 2. When Player 2 has run up and back to each line twice, Players 1 and 2 reverse roles. As players run faster and become more proficient, balls may be tossed with a little less arc. Any wild throws by the fielder are chased down by the fielder and that line is repeated.

9. Rundown situation without balls or basemen. Any number of players may participate at the same time. A player stands between two bases or marks. The coach blows a whistle or claps her hands and the player runs toward one base or mark. As the player nears her goal, the coach blows the whistle or claps her hands again, and the player reverses her direction and heads for the other goal. Each time the coach blows her whistle or claps her hands, the player changes direction.

10. Player 1 tosses the ball underhand and high toward Player 2, about 6 feet from her. Player 2 jumps up, extends her arms, and tries to catch the ball as high as possible. When Player 2 lands, she flexes her knees and hips, and brings the glove down to the floor or ground as though she were executing a tag play, and flips the ball back to Player 1. After ten repetitions, players reverse roles.

11. Player takes easy practice swings with a weighted bat.

COMMON SOFTBALL INJURIES
AND THEIR PREVENTION

Regardless of the precautions taken, abrasions, lacerations, and punctures of the skin will occur. Foreign objects, mainly dirt, will also find their way into eyes. Sprains, or injuries to the soft tissue—such as ligaments, tendons, and muscles—that surrounds the joints, will occur. Strains, particularly in the beginning of the season when athletes tend to overexert their muscles before they are fully conditioned, are another common ailment. Perhaps the most common forms of injury to the softball player are dislocations and fractures of fingers and ankles. Injuries to players cannot be entirely eliminated, but they can be substantially reduced in number and severity.

Attention to pre-season conditioning and a good general warm-up period before all practices and games can substantially reduce the number of strains suffered by players. Muscles, tendons, and ligaments that are strong and capable of stabilizing the joints they surround play an important role in preventing injuries to those joints.

Emphasis must be placed on both strength and flexibility since one without the other is dangerous to the athlete. Strong muscles with little flexibility may lead to numerous muscle-pull injuries. Very flexible muscles that don't have the necessary strength will cause dislocations rather easily. An athlete's overflexibility or lack of flexibility can be determined by observing her during warm-up exercises. An athlete who is able to touch her fingertips to the floor while bending from the waist and keeping her knees straight would probably be considered to possess an average amount of flexibility. If that athlete can place the palms of her hands flat on the floor in front of her feet, it would be prudent to assess the strength of her hamstring muscles and perhaps consider a strengthening program. However, an athlete who is not able to reach down past the tops of her ankles would be a candidate for hamstring flexibility exercises.

The flexibility of the elbows and wrist are two other important points to be considered. If the elbow hyperextends, the muscles that insert and originate on both sides of the joint should be assessed to see if they are strong enough to protect that joint from dislocation. An athlete whose elbow hyperextends and who must struggle to complete a half-dozen wrist curls with 5-pound weights would be wise to work on a strengthening program. Despite conditioning programs, muscles injuries can still occur. However, strong muscles have a better chance for a successful and complete recovery.

Selection of equipment that fits and is comfortable for the athlete can also prevent injury. Use of sneakers on black-top or cement surfaces and cleats or spikes on dirt and grass fields provides the athlete with better footing than ordinary street shoes. Uniforms that fit the athlete do not constrict her movement or get in her way when making a play. Headbands, barrettes, or other appurtenances that help keep hair from momentarily blinding or distracting an athlete are a simple but important safety factor. A catcher's gear, such as masks, body protectors, and shin guards, must fit the user. Masks or body protectors with stretched-out elastic straps can be more harmful than helpful. A catcher who wears glasses must find a mask that provides the best protection for the type of eyeglass frame she is wearing. Selecting a glove that the player can handle deftly is more important than using the largest glove available, since it may be too heavy or cumbersome. Utilization of a simple elastic strap to prevent eyeglasses from falling off or sliding down is also a safety factor. Cracked or split bats should be disposed of and not merely left in the bat bag for an over-anxious player to use.

Another important preventive technique that is commonly overlooked is a pre-game inspection of the playing facility by the coaches and/or players. Are there holes in the ground that can be filled? Are there stones or broken glass on the base paths or other areas where players may fall? Is there string, wire, branches, and so on in the grass that may tangle a player's feet? Are there jagged pieces of wood on the players' benches? Are sections of fencing broken or bent over, producing a dangerous area for players trying to catch foul balls? Are there mud puddles that may cause a player to slip and fall while pursuing a fly ball? Are the bases fastened securely?

Safety during pre-game warm-ups and during practice sessions is a must. Early emphasis on how to set up for throwing and batting practice is important. When players throw in twos, they should all throw parallel to one another rather than across or behind. It is better to turn and chase an errant throw than to have that throw hit a teammate. When more than one group is batting at the same time, care must be taken to avoid the danger of a cross-fire situation, with one group hitting into the other. The groups should be far enough apart to preclude foul balls or pulled balls being hit into the other group. Set up the practice so that players are not likely to chase balls into a roadway. Have players place spare equipment in suitable areas rather than leave it where others may step on it while chasing balls.

If the equipment used meets the needs of the athletes, if the field is in safe playing condition, and if the athletes are well conditioned, one of the most important remaining preventive measures is the teaching of good skills. If players will be sliding, have they been taught to slide properly? Does the infielder know how to cover her base safely for a tag play as well as for a force play? Do the fielders know that the baserunner has the right of way and that they must stay out of her path unless they are actually trying to tag her with the ball? Do baserunners pay attention to coaches for signals to stay up or slide? Do fielders know how to shade their eyes from the sun and call for fly balls? In general, are the players able to utilize good sound skills?

Teams that do not have the services of an athletic trainer, which is the vast majority of teams, often overlook the importance of reconditioning athletes after an injury. A sprained ankle, if treated properly, may cause a player to miss several games or, if she is permitted to return before she is ready, to play the remainder of the season at far less than peak efficiency. Once the pain and swelling has subsided, the athlete should begin a program of rehabilitation rather than immediately return to full participation. Since most amateur teams play once or twice a week, missing one or two more games will allow the athlete time to accommodate to full participation. In most cases, this requires cooperation between the athlete's physician and the coach in setting up a program of reconditioning with the athlete. Perhaps a program of easy jogging with wide circles and some light exercise might be a good beginning. Then the athlete can gradually build up to full running and participation depending upon the degree of pain and swelling. Icing down the affected area after participation is also helpful in preventing swelling. The physician may also suggest various types of support to protect the injured area.

A reconditioning period may be a source of frustration to the player anxious to return to action and the coach who would like to have her team at its maximum strength. However, an injury that is a thing of the past rather than a lingering source of aggravation is well worth the extra time required. One must remember that whether a player or a coach, the main reason for participation is the enjoyment received from it, and playing in pain or watching another person play in pain certainly detracts from that enjoyment.

FIRST-AID TREATMENT

Before first aid can be rendered to an injured athlete, certain basic materials must be available. It is important that each team carry with it an adequate first-aid field kit. Teams can purchase ready-made first-aid kits or, to keep expenditures down, may put together their own. A large coffee can, a metal cookie box, and a large plastic container are possible first-aid cases because they have tops that can be securely closed to keep out dirt and moisture. The following list may be helpful in organizing such a kit.

Adhesive tape. To hold gauze pads in place or to provide protective support for an injured area. Several rolls of varying widths are needed.

Antiseptic cream or spray. To aid in the healing and soothing of abrasions.

Bandages. For minor cuts. A variety of sizes should be included.

Cold packs. Chemical cold packs are a source of ice that can be carried, stored, and utilized when necessary. These cold packs may be used to reduce the amount of swelling that occurs after an injury.

Cotton or cotton swabs. To clean wounds and to apply an antiseptic.

Elastic bandages. To hold cold packs in place and to supply a source of compression to an injured area. Several rolls of varying widths should be included.

Eye cup and wash. To permit safe irrigation of an eye to extract dirt, and so on.

Foam rubber padding. To cushion bruises.

Gauze bandage. To hold gauze pads in place.

Peroxide. To clean abrasions, and so on.

Petroleum jelly. To prevent irritation from rubbing clothing, and so on.

Pre-tape or skin toughener. To protect the skin before adhesive tape is applied.

Safety pins. To anchor slings and help mend uniforms.

Scissors. To cut gauze and tape.

Sling. To immobilize an injured arm or shoulder.

Sterile gauze pads. To cover abrasions and lacerations and to clean wounds. A variety of sizes should be included.

Tongue depressors. To use as splints to immobilize suspected dislocated or fractured fingers.

Tweezers. To remove foreign particles, such as splinters, from wounds.

If an adequate field kit is available, the coach or another player may apply first aid to the injured athlete. It is important, however, to remember that although some coaches may be quite knowledgeable in the diagnosis of and care of injuries such as sprains and dislocations, trained medical personnel or paramedics should be consulted to accurately diagnose and properly treat injuries. Tape some coins to the inside cover of the field kit in case a phone call must be made to obtain medical assistance. The following are basic treatments for softball injuries.

Abrasions or scraping of the skin. Clean the wound as best as conditions permit, using soap and water or peroxide. Apply an antiseptic cream or spray to help prevent infection and cover with sterile gauze pads. Check daily for signs of infection.

Blisters. If an irritation is noticed before a blister actually develops, the area may be protected by applying a soft pad to prevent friction. If a blister has developed, clean the area thoroughly and then puncture the blister near its outer edge with a sterilized needle (use a match or alcohol to sterilize the needle) to permit the fluid to drain. Apply a sterile dressing to protect from infection. Check daily for signs of infection. If the blister is deep, under the skin, the athlete should consult a physician.

Bruises or contusions. Apply ice and a pressure bandage to minimize the swelling. A bruise on the shin or heel of the hand may require padding to protect the injury from repeated blows when the player returns to the game.

Dislocations. Immobilize the part and elevate it if possible. A tongue depressor may be used to immobilize a finger; a sling, for a shoulder. Take the athlete to a physician or emergency room for medical attention.

Fractures. If a fracture is suspected, the part should be immobilized and the player should be transported to a hospital for medical evaluation. Tongue depressors may be used to immobilize fingers; a sling may be used for a wrist, arm, or shoulder. Rolled-up blankets or magazines may be used to splint a leg. If fractures of the neck or spine are suspected, only trained personnel should move the injured athlete in order to avoid additional injury, including paralysis. With such suspected fractures, keep the athlete warm and quiet until help arrives.

Lacerations or jagged wounds. Clean the wound as best as conditions permit, then cover with a sterile dressing to prevent further contamination. The athlete should be taken to a physician as soon as possible to determine if there is foreign matter in the wound and if sutures are needed. If the wound was caused by a spike or cleat, a tetanus shot may be necessary.

Strains and sprains. Apply ice and immobilize the joint with an elastic bandage. Taping of the joint until it heals may be required. Depending upon the severity and the amount of swelling and pain, a physician should be consulted before the player is permitted to return to action.

Equipment

Use of expensive equipment will in no way ensure any player of a place on an all-star squad, but the selection of good quality, comfortable equipment will enhance her enjoyment of the game. The selection of one's personal equipment is a vital factor affecting one's performance and, more important, one's physical safety. A glove that is so small that the player is forced to catch the ball in the palm of the hand will not encourage a beginning player to reach out and make a stab at a hard line drive. On the other hand, a glove large enough to permit the ball to be caught in the webbing area may encourage that beginning player to take a stab at the ball no matter how fast it is traveling. In the first instance, the player may never have the opportunity to explore her own potential, while in the second, she may rise to stardom. In a similar vein, a shiny light-blue aluminum bat may be aesthetically appealing, but if that bat is too heavy to lift off the shoulder in time to meet the pitched ball, the hitter may dread her turn at bat and miss enjoying one of the most challenging aspects of the game.

Several general factors affect the choice of equipment a participant will purchase. The first concerns how serious about the sport she is. Will she utilize the equipment once a week or four or five times a week? If the player is considering play in an organized league where two, four, or more games are played per week, plus practice, she qualifies as a serious player and a higher quality of equipment is required to ensure durability. However, if the player is just beginning, and is perhaps not quite sure of the extent of her interest in the sport, a lower quality of equipment will do nicely.

The second factor is cost. Is the price of equipment inconsequential or an important consideration? Cost is important, particularly when one is purchasing a glove or shoes. The higher priced gloves and shoes are constructed with premium steerhide leather throughout, while the cheaper models substitute lower quality leathers and other fabrics. For recreational-level players, the cheaper equipment will provide good protection at a moderate cost.

The third factor is the set of regulations that apply to specific pieces of equipment. Is it legal? Can it be used in an official game? The official softball guides, published by the Amateur Softball Association and the National Association for Girls and Women in Sport, contain specific regulations concerning length and construction of bats, length of shoe spikes; types of gloves and mitts to be used by specific players; size, weight, and construction of balls; and specific protective equipment.

The fourth factor is the playing surface. Are the games played on dirt, blacktop, or concrete? Players participating in games played on dirt require shoes that have metal spikes or plastic or rubber cleats to provide a safe grip while running. Thick-soled sneakers, however, will provide safer footing and protection from the ground heat on blacktop or concrete surfaces.

The fifth factor is player comfort. Is that specific piece of equipment comfortable for that specific player to use? For many girls and women, little or youth league equipment such as body protectors and leg guards may provide a better fit than professional models designed for players over 6 feet tall. The same may hold true to some degree regarding gloves and shoes. It must also be kept in mind that there are specific body protectors designed for women, and that more suitable footwear, built to meet the needs of women players, have appeared on the market.

GLOVES AND MITTS

Official softball rules affect the type of gloves worn by players in various positions. Only the catcher and first baseman are permitted to wear mitts. A mitt is a form of glove that has one large area opposite the thumb, instead of individual fingers, and into which all four fingers are placed. It is sim-

Catcher's mitt

First baseman's mitt

ilar to a regular mitten in design, except for its greater size and padding.

Although players in these two positions are permitted to wear mitts, they may choose to wear regular softball/baseball gloves. If any other player used a mitt instead of a glove to catch a ball, that catch would be ruled illegal.

The mitt designed specifically for the catcher has a very heavily padded surface around the edges and gives a circular appearance. These mitts tend to be cumbersome and inflexible. Because of the difficulty in one-handing a softball with a conventional catcher's mitt, a catcher may choose to use a first baseman's mitt, which is more flexible and has a larger pocket area to better hold a softball. The ordinary fielder's glove has individual finger sections, usually three or four, and a thumb section. As in the mitt, the glove also has a webbing area between the thumb and index finger sections to facilitate catching and holding the ball. The fielder's glove also has a lacing along the top of the fingers, connecting the entire outer edge of the glove and making

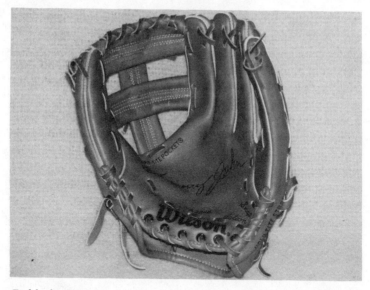

Fielder's glove

it possible for a comparatively small hand to use it with ease.

From time to time, manufacturers market gloves and mitts in various colors, such as red, blue, and white, in addition to the various shades of brown leather. Multicolor gloves or any one color are legal for all players except the pitcher. Only the pitcher's glove is mandated to be of one color, and cannot be either white or gray. Because of the confusion that could be caused by the resemblance to a ball, the glove worn by a softball player may not have any decorative white or gray circles on the outside.

In the past, gloves specifically labeled for softball were quite small and, thus, inadequate for their supposed function; that is, to protect the hand when a softball is being caught. Therefore the majority of softball players actually use baseball gloves. After all, a little common sense dictates that if one is going to use a glove to catch a ball larger than a baseball, one would not go to a smaller sized glove but would at least remain with one the same size as a baseball glove. With such innovations as the various types of lacing between the fingers and around the glove as a whole and the breaks in the heel, a relatively small hand can quite adequately control a relatively large glove. The important point to remember here is that a softball/baseball glove is not worn in the same manner as a glove being utilized to keep the hands warm. The fingers of the hand are not pushed into the glove so that the tip of each finger contacts the tip of the glove finger; rather, the heel of the hand rests upon the inside of the heel of the glove, and the fingertips are thus placed at the lower ends of the glove fingers, actually leaving the glove fingers almost empty. By merely flexing the fingers toward the thumb, the glove wraps around the ball in its pocket. Actually, by the "giving" action, or relaxation of the hand upon contact with the ball, the glove itself closes around the ball.

Despite all of the manufacturers' innovations, new gloves are still stiff and require a break-in period. Thus, when purchasing a new glove it is sometimes necessary to use the other hand to help shape the glove to help determine its comfort. Sometimes just applying a little pressure from behind with the other hand on the fingertips of the glove helps to establish the pocket and shows the comfort potential of the particular glove. One glove selection technique to avoid is selection based on the signature that appears on the glove. Whether the signature is that of your favorite ball player or of one you would love to see set a major-league record for being struck out the most number of times in any one season should not be considered in your selection. If the glove is what you want, if it feels comfortable, and if it is in your price range, that is the glove to purchase. Remember, the autograph will become covered with dirt and scuffed by the softball as base hit after base hit is snuffed out by that glove being in the right place at the right time.

The art of breaking in a glove varies, depending upon the experience of the individual. Some advocate rubbing the glove with a leather softener and then tying up a ball in the glove and letting it sit overnight. Others just like to tie a ball in the glove and let it sit. Some spend time pounding the pocket area with the fist to help develop the desired shape. Still others like to break in the glove by using it. The easiest and most effective method is a combination of the last two suggestions. Use the glove, catch with it. If you play medium- or fast-pitch ball, volunteer to warm up the pitcher. Although you may at first be the recipient of a rather odd look, when the new glove is spotted, the odd look will be replaced by one of comparative understanding. Then, when the game or practice session has been completed, place a ball in the glove and wrap the glove around the ball using heavy rubber bands to hold the glove in the desired position.

Once the glove has been broken in, occasionally wiping it with a damp cloth to remove the accumulation of dirt will not be harmful. Once the glove has been cleaned off, rub in a few drops of oil, such as neatsfoot oil, into the entire surface of the glove. This will extend the life of the glove by helping to prevent the leather from drying out, cracking, and scuffing. You will also notice that the oil from your hands also contributes to extending the glove's life. Another point to remember is that the glove or mitt was designed to catch softballs (or baseballs), not to serve as a pillow or seat cushion.

BATS

The use of either baseball or softball gloves and mitts is up to the preference of the player, with only minor restrictions imposed by the official rules. Baseball bats, however, are illegal in a softball game. A player using a baseball bat would have a decided advantage because of the difference in specifications.

A bat, whether wood or metal, must meet basically the same specifications. An overall length of 34 inches and a weight of 38 ounces are maximum. The diameter of the bat at its largest part cannot be greater than 2¼ inches. Wood bats must be manufactured from one piece of hardwood or from a block made by bonding several pieces of wood together. Metal bats must also be manufactured from one

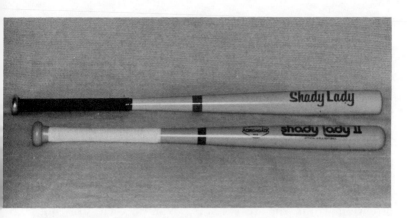

Official softball bats—metal and wood

Zapper—the bent-handled bat.

piece of tubing because rivets and wooden handles are not permitted. Both wood and metal bats must have a safety grip, 10 to 15 inches in length, extending from the small end of the bat; this grip may be composed of cork, tape, or other material. Every bat that is utilized in a regulation softball game must bear the manufacturer's "Official Softball" label.

Is there a bent bat in your future? The latest innovation in softball bats is just that, the bent-handled Zapper marketed by the Curley-Bates Company of California. According to the manufacturer, this unconventional styling will help in the development of a smoother and more powerful swing. Due to its unique design, the bat also enables the batter to swing faster and contact the ball earlier. Another feature of this bat is an improved alignment of the batter's arms and wrists that permit more efficient use of the back and forearm muscles. This last feature should definitely be a plus for women softball players because it is an acknowledged fact that the vast majority of women in the United States are deficient in upper body strength.

Bat selection can be difficult, particularly with the popularity of metal bats, which are available in a wide variety of colors and with names that can distract the purchaser's attention from the real issues. Names such as "Big Boomer," "Super Stick," "Hot Shot," "Thunder," "Fence Finder," and "Shady Lady" on bats colored lime green, peach, royal blue, purple, gold, orange, and light blue can easily attract the neophyte to a bat not at all suitable to that individual. Items of more importance are length, grip size, and weight. In medium- and fast-pitch leagues, these factors are even more significant than in slow pitch play.

A player with a small hand should look for a bat with a narrow grip to enable the hands to comfortably maintain a solid grip on the bat throughout the swing. A thicker grip may be more comfortable for a player with larger hands.

The weight of the bat is a prime consideration since the player must be able to swing the bat around in time to meet the pitch in front of the plate as well as to be able to check her swing if at the last minute the pitch seems out of the strike zone. A bat that is too heavy can cause the player to swing late or to swing in an uncontrolled manner. Although a heavier bat is capable of providing more power, the advantage is lost if the batter's timing is affected by the extra weight.

Length is also important. A bat that is too short can decrease a player's ability to hit outside pitches effectively, whereas a bat that is too long may cause a batter to contact a high percentage of pitches on the narrow part of the bat above the grip rather than on the fatter part of the barrel. A player's batting stance will also affect the choice of bat length. A longer bat may be more advantageous to a batter who stands farther from the plate than to one who crowds the plate.

Care of the bat is rather easy. Wiping it with a damp cloth to remove dirt and mud is a good practice. Cracks are easier to spot if the bat is fairly clean. Cracks not visible to the eye may be detected by holding the bat at the fat end of the barrel and tapping the small end on a solid surface. If the bat is cracked, the vibrations will travel the length of the bat. Using a cracked bat not only will lower a batter's average but is a dangerous practice for both the batter and those around her should the bat split on impact. The safety grips at the smaller end of the bat should be checked regularly for wear. Any grips that lose their effectiveness should be replaced immediately. Although it may not have the shock-absorbent quality of the original safety grip, plain adhesive tape can be used to provide a surface that the batter can grip securely. When using adhesive tape, however, care must be taken to avoid folds in the tape that could cause blisters to develop on the batter's hands.

Finally, remember that the bat was developed as an implement to be used in hitting softballs and not as a replacement hammer to drive stakes into the ground to hold down bases.

CATCHER'S PROTECTIVE EQUIPMENT

According to the official rules, women catchers who participate in fast-pitch leagues must wear both a mask and body protector, whereas those who participate in slow-pitch leagues are merely given the recommendation. Leg guards are neither required nor recommended by the rules for either fast- or slow-pitch softball.

There are body protectors with special cup-shaped molded breast protectors designed specifically for women. These special breast protectors may be attached to the inner (the side facing the player) surface of the body protector by side lacings or snaps, or may be permanently sewn on.

Depending upon the build of the individual player, body protectors with extra pads sewn in may be too cumbersome and may interfere with throwing and general movement. Also, the breast area is generally well protected by the glove. Those body protectors with the narrow pad over the throwing shoulder cause less interference when throwing than those with wide padding over both shoulders. In instances where the special women's body protectors are not available or perhaps are too large, Little League body protectors may provide a viable substitute. Although the rules require body protectors to be worn by catchers, women's models are not specified. Since both types of body protectors have adjustable straps, it is usually possible to adjust the straps to keep the protector close to the body; it will thus cause less interference and discomfort. When adjusting the straps, tighten the back strap sufficiently to pull the front of the protector up high enough to offer some

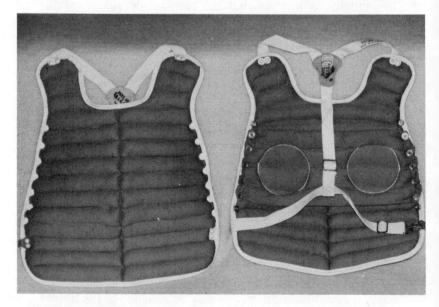

Women's body protector—outside and inside view

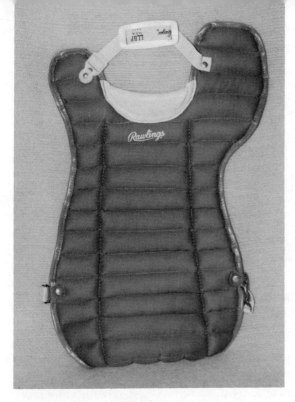

Regular body protector

protection to the throat area. Basic care simply consists of beating the accumulation of dust out of the protector and replacing neck and back straps when the originals have stretched out.

Softball masks are considerably lighter in construction than their baseball counterparts. Although lighter, softball masks have proven to offer more than adequate protection. When selecting a mask, the upper padding bar should rest against the forehead and the lower padding bar should rest on the chin. With the two padding bars thus positioned, the wearer should have an almost unobstructed view through the large opening. Again, straps are elastic and adjustable, and should be set to keep the mask padding in place against the forehead and chin.

For catchers who wear eyeglasses it is advisable to try out several masks before making a final selection. Some styles of catcher's masks offer better protection than others

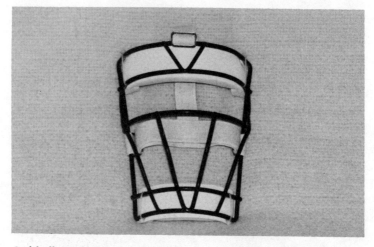

Softball mask

for various types of eyeglass frames. It is important to be sure that a corner of the eyeglass frame does not extend beyond the metal bars of the mask and remain vulnerable to foul balls.

Since the padded bars are either vinyl or vinyl covered, and the wire frame is also vinyl coated, cleaning is easy. Because the mask is worn to cover the face, frequent washing with warm soapy water keeps it clean. Straps and padding bars can be replaced to prolong the useful life of the mask.

Although not required in the regulations and currently not a widespread practice, softball catchers are beginning to wear batting helmets along with the mask for added protection from foul balls and errant bats. Major sporting goods companies such as Rawlings also market catcher's helmets designed specifically to protect the catcher's head. These helmets also have straps to which the mask can be attached.

An optional piece of equipment is leg guards. For both medium- and fast-pitch games, where catchers are going down on their knees to block pitches in the dirt, leg guards can save the catcher many bruises. Leg guards provide protection for the catcher's knees, shins, and insteps, and are attached by three straps. Some models also provide protection to the calf and ankle. Again, for girls and some women, Little League leg guards may provide a better fit and less interference with maneuverability. Care generally consists of wiping off the dirt and replacing stretched or torn straps.

Leg guards

SHOES

Shoes may be constructed of canvas, leather, or materials of a similar quality for the upper portion. If the spikes are no more than ¾ inch in length, regular metal heel and sole plates may be used. Soft or hard rubber cleats or smooth-soled shoes may also be worn, according to the official rules.

Until recently, regular baseball spikes or rubber Little League cleats were the only choices available to softball players who played on dirt. With the advent of synthetic turfs and the growth of interest in soccer in the United

Baseball spikes   *Rubber cleats*

States, a wide selection of multipurpose shoes became available in both boy's and men's sizes. These shoes may have uppers made of nylon, vinyl, and army duck canvas instead of the calfskin, soft cowhide, and high-grade split leather uppers of the conventional shoes. The multipurpose shoes have molded soles of various grades of plastic and rubber. As the shoes go up in cost, items such as the padded tongue, collar, and heel, as well as arch supports, are more visible and of better quality. Those players who play on blacktop or concrete should look to a good grade, thick-soled sneaker. Options such as the padded tongue, heel, collar, and arch supports are of equal importance for the sneaker wearer. The Achilles heel guard is another worthwhile option.

Although more shoes designed for women are beginning to appear on the market, the vast majority are manufactured for boys and men. These shoes run wider, and a woman would take approximately one full size smaller than her normal shoe size. The extra width, to a degree, has an advantage in that it permits the toes to spread while the player is running. Since all shoes are required to be laced up, they can usually be made tight enough to be comfortable. Another advantage is that since the shoes are perhaps wider than those normally worn, the player has room to wear two pairs of socks. One pair is usually a fairly thin cotton sock worn next to the foot; the second pair, a thick athletic sock, is worn over the first. This two-sock technique should help reduce foot slippage, provide more padding, absorb more perspiration, and help prevent blisters.

An option applicable to pitchers is the toe plate. This is a small piece of metal molded to slip on the front of the shoe, part under the sole and part above. Usually, this piece is riveted to a piece of leather. The toe plate is attached to the sole with several small screws, and the leather part has eyelets that are held in place by regular laces. Use of the toe plate prevents wear on the toe area of the shoe that most pitchers drag off the rubber after the ball is released.

Care of softball shoes is similar to that of any other shoe: clean and polish them. In addition, the accumulation of dirt and grass should be dug out of the sole cleats, keeping the spikes or cleats ready to carry out their designed function.

*Multipurpose
shoes*

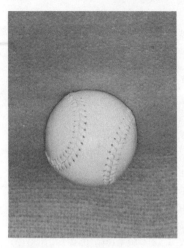 

Regular or baseball seam softball   *Hidden stitch softball*

BALLS

Softballs must meet the standards set by the International Joint Rules Committee. A tolerance of ¼ inch is permitted in the circumference of a softball, a variance of 11⅞ to 12⅛ inches. The weight of an official softball may vary from 6¼ to 7 ounces. Top-quality horsehide or cowhide is used to construct the outer cover of the ball.

The stitching on the balls is basically of two varieties. The first is similar to that of baseballs. The second is a hidden stitch seam. Teams that play and practice on dirt fields use softballs that have the regular baseball-type stitching. Teams that play on hard or abrasive surfaces such as blacktop and concrete usually use the hidden seam ball because the rougher surface will not come into direct contact with the stitching thread.

Although not used in official softball games, rubber covered softballs are available to use for practice on fields where rainy weather creates slow draining puddles and/or where dampness is a problem. Rubber covered softballs also wear well when used in pitching machines. For indoor use, particularly in small gymnasium areas, restricted flight balls or fleece balls are safer to use than official softballs, particularly for batting. Soft softballs with sponge rubber and cork centers are also practical for indoor use.

UNIFORMS

The uniform worn by a team must be of the same color and style for each player. For women, uniforms consisting of shorts and shirts are perhaps the most popular. Satin uniforms at one time were the thing, but today, a variety of easy-care, polyester, double-knit fabrics are available, and polyester has assumed the lead in popularity. Appropriate softball uniforms designed for women are manufactured by a large number of sporting goods companies. Matching knee socks usually finish out the uniform. If teams play their games at night, knickers may be more appropriate than shorts. Whether shorts or knickers, uniforms made of easy-care fabrics are available in a wide variety of colors and shades with contrasting trims. With the increased popularity of gym shorts and T-shirts among the entire population, teams short of money could probably outfit a team at a local department store for a nominal sum.

Teams that play games during evenings or in the early spring may also wear long-sleeved shirts under the uniform shirt for additional warmth. These shirts may be regular long-sleeved turtleneck shirts or the regular baseball/softball undershirt with a light gray or natural colored body and sleeves to match the uniform. As part of a uniform, these shirts must be identical for each player. For those players who slide often, sliding pants or pads may be worn under the uniform pants. These pads cover and protect a player's hips and sides, and are usually made of quilted cotton material. Athletic and protective bras are now available through manufacturers of women's sporting equipment.

A jacket may round out the uniform. Depending on the weather of the area, the jackets may range from light nylon windbreakers to lined twill and satin jackets. Again, if they are issued as part of the uniform, they should be identical for all players.

SCOREBOOKS

Scorebooks are necessary, since each team must present and follow a specific line-up. Whether a team employs an official team scorer or players on the bench keep the score, a uniform set of symbols and scoring techniques is necessary. If the players, coaches, and managers, as well as the official team scorer, can read and decipher the scorebook, they can all gain valuable information. The official rule book provides guidelines for judging assists, errors, hits, put-outs, and who is the winning or losing pitcher.

MISCELLANEOUS EQUIPMENT

Ball bags, bat bags, bases, home plates, and pitcher's plates are some other pieces of equipment a team may have to supply. Specially designed ball and bat bags may be purchased to carry equipment, or ordinary canvas duffle bags and various sized canvas and plastic bags may be substituted. An official home plate has five sides, and is constructed of rubber or similar material. The three bases are constructed of canvas or a similar material, and may be vinyl covered. They are 15 inches square and may not be thicker than 5 inches. The pitcher's plate may be either wood or rubber and is 6 inches wide and 24 inches long. If a team must supply the bases, it should also keep a hammer with the bases to drive the stakes into the ground to attach the bases. A 100-foot metal tape measure should also be available. If a tape measure cannot be purchased, heavy cord, with large knots at the end, at 60 feet, and again at 120 feet, can provide a cheap measure for accurately laying out the bases. Another knot, at a distance of 40 feet, will provide an accurate measure of distance from the rear of home plate to the front of the pitcher's plate.

Coaching or learning aids such as batting "tees" for youngsters and pitching machines are other examples of equipment teams may purchase. Batting helmets, running helmets, drag mats, rosin bags, and batting gloves are samples of additional small equipment items a team or individual player may purchase.

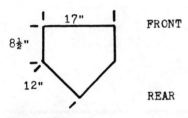

Home plate

Organizing to Play

PRESEASON CONSIDERATIONS

When considering the prospect of coaching a team there are many things that must be studied and arranged. Besides a basic knowledge of the game, the prospective coach must be aware of league or association rules regarding game procedures as well as those that govern the conduct of players and coaches. If the league or association has seasonal or organizational meetings, it is imperative that the prospective coach attend. In this way she will gain first-hand knowledge of the rules and regulations and will have the advantage of asking pertinent questions. Scheduling can be carried out at such meetings, or the prospective coach may be handed a schedule arranged by the athletic director or the association person in charge of the softball program.

Even teams composed of players who possess excellent skills and are well coached suffer injuries. The coach must see that adequate first-aid treatment will be available. Also, whether the individual players, a team registration fee, or the association or sponsor under whose auspices the team

184

will play pays the bill, the team should carry player insurance. Related to this are requirements of medical examination forms and/or parent consent forms. Although it is a good policy, probably only teams under the auspices of educational institutions will require submission of the above forms.

Teams must also be outfitted. Whether school teams, association teams, or specific league teams, there are uniform requirements to enable officials to distinguish the players of one team from those of the other. Uniforms may be as simple as a specific shade of T-shirt with a specific color short or dungarees, or they may be full regulation softball uniforms. Depending on the funding of the particular team, the individual players may have to arrange to supply their own uniform or the sponsoring organization may supply them on a lending basis. Whatever the source of the uniforms, the coach must also be aware of the possibility of uniform infractions prohibiting the participation of the offending player or team.

Although in most instances players supply their own gloves and shoes, game and practice balls, bats, bases, catcher's gear, and playing facilities must also be provided. Umpire fees are another game-related expense. If games are played on a home-and-away basis rather than on a league or association field, the coach must know who provides the transportation. The same is true if there are overnight trips, tours, and championship tournaments. In conjunction with the latter, tournament entry fees are another consideration. In school situations, the educational institution provides these fees; the sponsoring organization, whether one firm or donations from many small businesses, covers the expenses for "outside" teams. Admission charges for games and various fund-raising projects may also be used to defray expenses. Whatever the case, the coach must be aware of the funding of the team before she meets the players.

Once the basic organizational items have been arranged, the coach can begin to set up a tryout program. When the coach is not sure of the range of ability levels with which she will be dealing, or even if she knows that the ability level is quite high, a tryout program is more successful and safer if adequate supervision is provided. Since time is usually an important concern, people must be evaluated as quickly and accurately as possible to facilitate the organization of a practice schedule that will meet the group's ability and needs. If there is no specific assistant coach involved, the coach may gain assistance by enlisting several older, more experienced players or retired players.

Knowing which practice facility is available and when, the coach can begin arrangements to contact prospective players. The auspices under which the team plays affects the specific form the recruitment takes, but there are many general means that may be adapted to industry, educational institutions, or outside teams. Posters in store windows, employee meeting areas, and hallways of schools and churches aid in contacting specific populations. Local newspapers are other means of reaching prospective players. Flyers and throwaways that can be put in mailboxes or on car windshields are another means of advertising. Word of mouth—that is, talking to known players or coaches who may know of others not affiliated with a specific team or who had played for disbanded teams—is another means of contacting players.

Hand-out material, sign-up sheets, and name tags are other items for the coach to prepare. Information sheets to be handed out at the end of the tryout session may include information such as: name and phone number of the person to contact if a player is ill or unable to participate in a particular practice; list of player responsibilities; tentative practice schedule as well as game schedules, if available; uniform requirements and regulations; and necessary league or institution forms that must be completed and returned. Several sign-up sheets, together with pens and clipboards, help in securing accurate basic player information such as name, address, phone number, age, position, car availability, and so on. Name tags, whether sticker type or oaktag circles attached with cord and pins, on which players can print their first names will help get things going and make the tryout session more organized and enjoyable for all.

Although you may not know exactly how many players will attend the tryouts, you must make plans to organize the two- or three-hour session to obtain the maximum benefit. A brief introduction of yourself and your assistants is a good way to start. Then explain the team as you visualize it, the level of competition, the specific league in which the team will play, travel arrangements, game and practice information. In general, explain your aspirations for the team and your expectations of the players. This may be followed by some general conditioning and then various specific skill drills or activities geared to help assess the ability of the players to provide the information necessary to organize effective practices. The drill activities must be arranged around the personnel available to assist as well as the number of balls and bats and the size of the practice facility. The drills will have to be flexible enough to be adapted to the number of players who attend.

TRYOUTS

After having spent hours formulating letters to individuals or institutions, making phone calls, designing posters, and preparing flyers to announce your team tryouts, the fateful day finally arrives. Shortly after you enter your designated gymnasium or softball field, you find yourself facing perhaps twenty or so strange faces. Each of the twenty prospective players is curious about twenty other people, the other nineteen players and you.

If you are fortunate enough to have several assistant coaches or volunteers, you can begin by requesting that all those interested in pitching and catching go to a particular area with one assistant, those interested in the outfield with another assistant, and infielders with the third assistant. In the smaller groups, the assistant coach can help introduce the members of the group while they fill out the information sheets. As they print their names and addresses, the assistant can print their names on the name tags. Although it may take a few minutes to make up name tags, they pay for themselves when you are able to speak to players by name. The tags will make it easier for coaches to associate the faces and names of players and to assess players' abilities correctly. They also help players to get to know other players.

Once the basic formalities of finding out who is who are over, the next step is to find out who can do what. Perhaps the group will once again get together as a whole and one of the assistants may lead them in some warm-up activities such as a little easy jogging followed by some specific stretchies for various parts of the body. Then, depending upon the equipment available, the assessment of skills begins. If there are enough balls, everyone may take a partner and, in twos, the group may warm up by throwing and catching. After some general throwing and catching, the players can be requested to throw ground balls or fly balls to one another. During this time, the coaches may walk around offering assistance where needed and praise where deserved. Several batting groups can now be set up, one under the direction of each assistant. If tryouts are on a field, regular batting can take place with players taking turns pitching or throwing overhand to the batters. If the tryouts are in a gymnasium, players set up in twos or in small groups for bunting and fielding.

One group at a time goes through some baserunning demonstrations. On a signal from a coach, individual players take an imaginary swing at an imaginary pitch and run to first base to beat out an imaginary single. The coach times each runner or just observes the technique utilized. After two or three trials, players are asked to circle the bases. Again, their runs may be timed as well as observed for technique.

After all have had an opportunity to bat and run, a coach can take her outfielders and have them shag fungo fly balls. Another coach can set up a basic infield workout by hitting ground balls to players and having them throw to a player on first base or just back to a catcher standing next to the coach. The third coach can have the pitchers pitch to one another.

If the players are inexperienced, a brief demonstration and explanation should precede each type of skill assessment. During the entire tryout, the basic information clipboards should be passed from coach to coach with each group. By folding the sheet over so that just the name remains visible, each coach will have room to jot down a pertinent comment or two about each player she sees. Then, at the post-tryout meeting, a fairly accurate assessment of skill level as a whole and on an individual basis is possible.

When the basic tryout period is over, the group assembles again as one unit. Some positive remarks about the experience in general will reinforce the interest demonstrated. Reminders of the responsibilities of the individual players to work hard, be on time, get into condition, and return parent consent forms or medical forms, if applicable, are appropriate. Institution or league regulations regarding players and teams may be briefly reviewed. The session can be brought to a close with the announcement of the time, place, and date of the next meeting, and the distribution of handout material.

In situations where equipment is limited, players should rotate activities. One group could bat using several different sized bats and two or three balls. At the same time a coach, using one bat and one or two balls, could hit to another group. A third group of eight or ten players could throw in twos using four or five balls. In this instance, tryouts could be run with only twelve to fifteen balls and three or four bats. If balls are more limited in number, one group using no softballs could work on running skills while the other groups use the limited supply of balls.

PRACTICE

Once an assessment of the players' abilities has been made, practice sessions should be planned. Regardless of the skill level of the players, a certain amount of time is always allocated to the basics of throwing, fielding, and batting. However, the less experienced the players, the more time must be devoted to learning and improving the basic skills.

Each practice should begin with a warm-up period. This may consist of jogging and stretchies, followed by game-related activities. A thorough pre-practice warm-up will substantially decrease the number of sore arms and legs, as well as contribute to the general fitness level of the team members. A coach may lead or direct this phase of the practice for the first several meetings, after which warm-ups may be turned over to a designated team member or everyone on a rotating basis. In situations where the coach has no assistants, this helps to relieve her of some of the more routine aspects.

Following a warm-up period of approximately fifteen to twenty minutes, work on the basic throwing, catching, bunting, batting, and baserunning techniques should begin. By assigning players on a rotating basis to set out bases and equipment, the coach can eliminate another routine activity. This provides the players with more responsibility and also gives them the opportunity to contribute to the team effort in another way.

After the basic skills have been worked on, the next major section of the practice should involve the combined infield and outfield for general team play. Besides fielding ground balls, catching fly balls, and the subsequent throws to appropriate bases, time is spent on a variety of double plays, base coverage under various conditions, relay systems, and the backing up of each position.

Extra players may be rotated into positions. When not participating in the actual field practice, other players can run sprints, play pepper, or work on specific weaknesses off to the side in foul ground. Extra players can also be used as baserunners at this time. While they get the baserunning experience, the fielders learn to field and throw around baserunners.

The last fifteen or twenty minutes can be spent in a game-like scrimage. If the roster is sufficiently large, two teams can be set up. Because many teams are permitted to outfit only fifteen or sixteen players, the team should be divided into three groups with one group at bat while the other two are in the field. To speed play, generally, batters are allowed only two or three swings rather than the official number of balls and strikes, and only two outs per team are permitted.

INDOOR PRACTICE

Most teams do not have fieldhouse facilities and, therefore, must restructure their practice sessions when forced to practice indoors. Many of the same drills utilized on an outdoor field can be adapted to indoor facilities by using soft softballs or by throwing balls instead of batting them.

Although most indoor facilities are not large enough to set up an entire field, it is often possible to utilize bases in an infield set-up. This can turn into a good opportunity to sharpen baserunning techniques for offensive play and to improve the defense against such plays as the first and third situation or a runner stealing second on the pitch and going to third on the bunt.

While regular batting practice is not safe in most indoor settings, bunting usually presents no safety problems. When golf nets or cushioned walls are available to absorb the impact of a batted ball, batters can hit balls tossed from the side into the impact-absorbing material. If a pitching machine is available, it can be set up inside a golf net to permit a batter to safely take regular batting practice in a confined area.

Depending upon the age level, plastic bats and balls may be utilized indoors. Such equipment permits game-like situations on a smaller scale. This provides inexperienced ball players with the opportunity to learn when to tag up or when to play the lead runner. Although plastic balls may be hit quite hard, they do not have the same force as regulation softballs. Also, the plastic bats, being very light, pose little danger should anyone be accidently hit by one.

Of course, indoor practice lends itself to discussion of rules because of the ease of communication. Chalkboards and magnetic boards can be used to illustrate rules. Live demonstrations, even with bases on a smaller scale than the official distance, can be used to show the correct way to return to first base after running out a single or how to legally take a lead with a pitch.

GAMES

Organizing for games involves more than merely having a team show up an hour before game time. Of course, it is important to have your team there, in uniform and prepared to play, but consideration of field conditions, umpires, and equipment is also necessary.

If your team is the home team, adequate arrangements for a field must be made. To reserve most fields, a permit must be obtained in order to ensure use of the particular field at a specified time. Arrangements must be made concerning who is responsible for lining the field and setting out the bases. If lights are needed, you must know where and how they are turned on. Teams that use public address systems must provide for reliable announcers as well as make sure that the equipment will be adequately set up. Besides being aware of the legal aspects involved in charging admission to or collecting donations during the game at a particular field, you must have reliable personnel on hand to carry out this duty.

In order to hold an official game, umpires are required. In some situations the individual home team is responsible for scheduling its own officials; in other instances, leagues provide officials for all league games. Method of payment must also be decided before the season begins. If the requirement is that umpires are paid before the game begins, money must be available, or if a league fee covers this expense, the coach may only have to sign a card for verification.

The home team is also responsible for providing accurate travel directions to the visiting teams and officials. This can be done by submitting one copy of directions to a league official, who in turn duplicates and sends a full set of directions to all teams and officials, or by each individual team.

As a visiting team, travel decisions must be made. Does the team travel as a unit, in a three- or four-car motorcade, or do players get there on their own? In either case, a time requirement for travel is necessary to ensure arrival on time. Trips requiring several hours of driving time must also allow for rest and snack stops.

Whether the home or visiting team, each team should have one person responsible for keeping the scorebook. This is necessary not only to maintain the proper batting order but also to check on the opposing team and to supply information to aid in organizing team defense.

Besides providing for the availability of catching gear, bats, and practice balls, the home team must also provide game balls. Game balls must be official softballs that meet league requirements. Generally, two or three new balls are required for each game. It doesn't hurt to have one or two spare game balls just in case one gets lost, cut, or soaked.

Last, but not least, don't forget that pre-game check of the field for dangerous conditions. If a portion of the fence is cut or bent so that it presents a potential danger to a fielder, a ground rule to protect the players may be established before the game begins. Should broken glass or other extraneous material be noticed on the field, it can be removed before the game begins. Rules may also be devised to cover holes in the fence and any other problem that cannot be eliminated before a game time.

LEAGUES

The main function of a league is to encourage play on an organized basis. Some leagues were formed out of the desire of coaches to provide for more equalized competition and better scheduling of games. League play usually involves teams in a home-and-away schedule. This type of play also affords teams a more approachable goal, for example, a league championship as opposed to much larger state or regional championships. Other leagues are organized with the intent of bringing together the strongest teams in a large geographical area involving a number of different states.

All leagues, regardless of their scope, have governing rules or a constitution that promotes uniform handling of any situation that may arise. Such rules serve as guidelines for dealing with forfeits, scheduling changes, field standards, team responsibilities, officiating, insurance, and player regulations. League officials, their responsibilities and tenure of office, and such considerations as dues to cover mailings, publicity, and awards are also spelled out.

Other organizations, for example, city or town recreation departments, the local YMCA, or the Catholic Youth Organization, sponsor leagues for school-age players. Such leagues often adapt the official softball rules to better meet the needs and abilities of their participants. Length of games, pitching and base distances, stealing bases, and sliding are some of the areas where such organizations may deviate from the official rules.

The Catholic Youth Organization of the Diocese of Rockville Centre for many years has operated an extremely successful softball program for girls. Their program divides the girls by age into five divisions, the Junior, Intermediate, Teen, Tyro, and Senior divisions. The three youngest divisions play with some rule modifications aimed at making the game meet the ability level of the participants, whereas the two older divisions play under official softball rules. The regulations cover uniforms, inclement weather, behavior, length of game, and some special considerations. A copy of these rules and regulations begins on page 201.

OTHER ORGANIZATIONS

At the collegiate level, there are two associations that govern women's softball at four-year institutions and one at the two-year college level. The Association for Intercollegiate Athletics for Women (AIAW) has been concerned solely with women's intercollegiate sports since its inception. The National Collegiate Athletic Association (NCAA), which has a long history of governing men's intercollegiate athletics, has recently become involved in women's intercollegiate athletics. The National Junior Collegiate Athletic Association (NJCAA) is the equivalent of the AIAW and NCAA on the two-year-college level. These associations set basic eligibility rules and sponsor championship tournaments. They also specify the number of scholarships for athletes per sport.

Intercollegiate competition is provided on three different levels—Division I, Division II, and Division III. These divisions permit colleges to participate on their own level in terms of scholarships offered and competition desired.

At the high school level, there are city and state associations that determine standards for interscholastic competition.

The Amateur Softball Association (ASA) is an organization totally dedicated to softball. Besides being involved in rule development and revision, the ASA organizes tournaments for both men and women at the city through national levels. National tournaments are conducted every year in both fast- and slow-pitch in the Major Division, Class A Division, 15-and-Under Division, and the 18-and-Under Division. Additional slow-pitch tournaments are conducted for the Industrial and Church divisions. There are also national championships in 16″ Slow Pitch, Modified Pitch, and Co-Ed softball. In 1982, for the first time national championships were held for the 12-and-Under Division.

The ASA sponsors clinics for umpires, coaches, and players. All ASA registered teams receive a copy of *Balls and Strikes,* the official publication of the ASA, and a copy of the *Official Guide and Rule Book.* The ASA also offers other printed material on various facets of the game and provides films on a loan basis. The ASA national office is located at 2801 N.E. 50th Street, Oklahoma City, Oklahoma 73111. The names of local commissioners may be obtained from the national office.

The National Association for Girls and Women in Sport (NAGWS), a branch of the American Alliance for Health, Physical Education, Recreation, and Dance, serves women's sports, including softball. This association develops guidelines for the conduct of sports programs for girls and women, aids in the training and rating of officials, disseminates research and information concerning women's sports, and publishes rulebooks, scorebooks, and articles on the various aspects of sports. Publications lists are available from: AAHPERD Publication, Dept. V, P.O. Box 870, Lanham, Maryland 20801.

Published from April through September, *Womens Softball,* is a magazine devoted to reporting the current news in the sport. It prints articles and pictures on collegiate softball teams as well as ASA teams. Tournament information, special feature articles, and advertisements for specific softball equipment are also to be found in this publication, which is available by writing Dorothy Davis, Editor, 256 S.W. Tualatin Loop, West Linn, Oregon 97068.

Two other magazines, *Women's Coaching Clinic* and *Coaching: Women's Athletics,* regularly publish articles on various facets of the sport of softball. They are available, respectively, from Prentice-Hall, Inc., Englewood Cliffs, New Jersey 07632 and Intercommunications, Inc., 1353 Boston Post Road, Madison, Connecticut 06443.

Although not geared specifically to softball, *The First Aider,* is a publication that deals with the care and prevention of athletic injuries in general. The articles vary from month to month, providing information that can be applied to athletes participating in a variety of sports. This magazine is available through Cramer Products, Inc., P.O. Box 1001, Gardner, Kansas 66030.

Glossary

Base path. An area 3 feet to either side of a line that goes from one base to another.

Batter's box. The areas located to the left and right of home plate, 3 feet wide and 7 feet long. They are located 6 inches to either side of home plate and designate the area in which the batter must stand when it is her turn to bat.

Batting order. The order in which the players on a team must bat.

Catcher's box. A continuation of the outside lines of the batter's box, 10 feet in length and 8 feet, 5 inches in width. The area in which the catcher must be located when the pitcher is ready to pitch.

Coach's box. A 15-foot line located in foul ground, 8 feet from either foul line. The line runs from a point opposite first and third bases toward home plate. The area in which the coaches must stand to direct the action of their team.

Count. The number of balls and strikes on the batter.

Double. A hit that permits the batter-baserunner to safely reach second base without the aid of an error.

Down. The number of outs.

Extra-base hit. A hit that allows the batter-baserunner to reach second or third base safely without the aid of an error.

Fair ball. A batted ball that hits first or third base, is touched by a fielder within the infield area, or bounces within the foul line past first and third.

Force out. A means of recording an out when a fielder has possession of the ball at a base to which the baserunner must run before that baserunner reaches that base. Throwing the batter-baserunner out at first base is a typical force out.

Foul ball. A ball that first touches an object or player outside of the foul lines, not in fair ground. It is counted as a strike on the batter if the batter has less than a two-strike count.

Fungo hit. Technique whereby a ball is tossed up and hit by the batter. Generally employed to provide outfielders with practice fielding fly balls.

"Giving" action. Pulling in or collapsing of the glove toward the body as the ball is caught in order to absorb the impact.

Hole. The space between two fielders that is not covered by either.

Home team. The team on whose field the game is being played. Also the team that bats in the second half of the inning.

Lead-off batter. The first batter to bat in the inning.

Line drive. A hard-hit ball that travels, with little arc, almost parallel to the ground.

Obstruction. The act of a fielder, without the ball, getting into a baserunner's way.

Pepper. Played with one batter and one or more fielders. The batter either bunts at or takes a half swing at the ball tossed by the fielder immediately after she fields the ball.

The ball is continually thrown, batted, and fielded in rapid succession.

Pitcher's plate. A rubber or wood slab 2 feet long and 6 inches wide, located near the center of the infield, 40 feet from the point of home plate. Marks the point where the pitcher must begin her motion.

Pop-up. A short fly ball hit within the infield or in the related foul ground.

Presenting the ball. Action by the pitcher just prior to beginning her pitching motion. She stands with both feet on the pitcher's plate and ground with the ball in both hands.

Run and hit. A play in which the baserunner leaves with the pitch in anticipation of the batter hitting a base hit.

Sacrifice. A batter who gives herself up to advance a baserunner.

Scoring position. A runner or runners on second or second and third.

Shag. Chasing down and catching batted fly balls during batting or fielding practice.

Single. A hit that permits the batter-baserunner to safely reach first base without the aid of an error.

Taking the pitch. A pitch that a batter does not swing at.

Three-foot line. A line 30 feet long, 3 feet from the first base foul line, extending from first base toward home plate. It designates the area where the batter-baserunner should run as she approaches first base.

Triple. A hit that permits the batter-baserunner to safely reach third base without the aid of an error.

Visiting team. The team playing on the opponents' home field. Also, the team that bats in the top half of the inning.

Catholic Youth Organization Softball Rules and Regulations

(Revised Spring 1980)
As used by the Catholic Charities Diocese
of Rockville Centre, New York

The General Policies and Procedures for CYO Competitive
Programming, revised 9/79, cover all CYO Programs. Your
attention is directed to them and these specifics for softball.

1. Eligibility commences with the Junior Division.
2. A parish may enter in each division as many teams
   as it is able to field.
3. Eighteen (18) players is the maximum number a
   team may carry on its roster. Fifteen (15) is the recommended minimum but it is not a requirement.
4. First base must be staked down. Second and Third
   bases may not be staked down.
5. Junior and Intermediate Divisions:
   Pitching Distance 33 feet Baselines 50 feet
   Teen Division:
   Pitching Distance 35 feet Baselines 55 feet
   Tyro, Senior Divisions:
   Pitching Distance 40 feet Baselines 60 feet

6. The visiting team has the responsibility to check the playing field and accept it as playable—pitching distance, baseline distances, prior to the official start of the game.

7. Bats must be Little League or marked, "Official Softball." Each bat must have a safety grip of cork, tape, or composition material 10" to 15" from the narrow handle end.

8. Sliding is permissible in all divisions.

9. There is no bunting, stealing, or advancing on a dropped third strike in the Junior, Intermediate and Teen Divisions. A base runner may NOT advance if the catcher commits an error catching the pitched ball and the ball gets past the catcher. A base runner may attempt to advance if the pitcher commits an error on the throw-back from the catcher.

10. (A) Seven (7) innings or 1½ hours, whichever comes first, will constitute an official game. No new inning may commence 1 hour and 25 minutes after the start of the contest. If conditions should warrant, in the judgment of the official, five (5) innings will constitute an official ball game.

    (B) Prior to the official start of the game, the official and competing coaches must synchronize watches.

11. In the event of a TIE at the expiration of the game (7 innings or 1½ hours, whichever comes first), ONE extra inning will be played. If the game is still tied at the end of the one extra inning, the game is *over*. It must then be rescheduled with both coaches arriving at a mutually agreeable: date, time and place. Both teams shall equally divide the officials' fees. *Home coach* notify the CYO Office with details.

12. If inclement weather should develop during a game, a decision must be made to continue or terminate within one-half hour. Any part of the suspended time is not to be considered as playing time or a part of the 1½ hours previously stated.

13. (A) On a day where it has rained PRIOR to game

time (on that day) and the field is NOT playable, coaches can agree to play on adjacent area, if coaches and official agree that area is not too wet and dangerous. If either coach objects to playing the game it will be postponed.

(B) On a day when it HAS NOT rained prior to game time but field is unplayable due to previous inclement weather, teams MUST play on adjacent area and will not have option to postpone game.

14. All playoff games in the Championships will be played to completion with no time limit.

15. The catcher must wear a face mask and body protector. Only the catcher and first baseman may wear mitts. The catcher and first baseman may wear gloves. All other players wear gloves.

16. Sneakers or rubber cleats must be worn.

17. All players must present a well-groomed, uniform team appearance. (A) Shorts, dungarees, culottes or slacks must be worn and whichever is chosen, ALL members of the team must wear them and they must be of the same color and style. A team may change from one to the other if it so wishes relative to weather conditions.

(B) Blouses or tee shirts must be worn and whichever is chosen, ALL members of the team must wear them and they must be of the same blend or match in color and style.

(C) Numbers will be sewn or pressed on the back, front, side, sleeve or wherever the team wishes to wear them but ALL members must wear said numbers in the same place.

(D) Caps as a part of the uniform are optional. If one player wears a cap then ALL members should wear a cap with the exception of the catcher. Caps must be of the same color and style.

(E) If weather is sufficiently inclement, necessitating additional clothing, a sweater, sweat shirt or jacket may be worn until such time as the weather warms.

18. The official will hold the coach of a team as respon-

sible for the behavior of any individual sitting on the bench of that team and in addition the home team coach will be held responsible for the playing atmosphere. Foul language on the part of coaches, officials, players or spectators will not be tolerated under penalty of default.

19. A forfeit will be declared if a team is unable to field nine (9) players within 15 minutes of the scheduled time.

20. Two (2) forfeits will disqualify a team from further league activity.

21. If not otherwise stated, CYO SOFTBALL will operate under the current rules of the National Association for Girls and Women in Sports. *

---

*
An up-to-date copy of the Official Playing Rules of the Amateur Softball Association of America can be purchased at sporting goods stores or by mail from the Amateur Softball Association of America (2801 N.E. 50th St., Oklahoma City, OK 73111).

Index

abrasions, first aid for, 162
Amateur Softball Association
  (ASA), 1, 2, 195–96
ankle weights, 153
arm, stretching exercises for, 149–
  51
arm motions
  in running, 24, 25
  in throwing, 10–13, 20
Association of Intercollegiate
  Athletics for Women
  (AIAW), 195

back, stretching exercises for,
  147–49
back-up responsibility
  in bunt defense, 71
  of catcher, 130–31
  drills for, 57
  of infielders, 56–57
  of outfielders, 54–56
  of pitcher, 118
  in rundown play, 66
  in team concept, 136–37
ball(s)
  bad bounce by, 20
  bounce point of, 46
  fear of being hit by, 20–21
  flight of, 24
  game, 193
  grip on. See grip
  presentation of, 105–6
  selection of, 180–81
  spin of, 114–16
Balls and Strikes (American
  Softball Association), 196

base hit, bunt for, 86–87
baseman
  at first, 30–34
  position play drills for, 40–44
  responsibilities of, 27–28
  at second, 34–38
  starting positions of, 28–29
  at third, 38–40
base running
  drills for, 101–3
  on extra-base hit, 93
  return to base from, 96
  signals in, 92
  single, 92–93
  sprint in, 91
  stride in, 96–101
  taking lead and, 94–95
bases
  construction of, 182
  layout of, 182–83
bases-loaded situation, catcher in,
  129
bat(s)
  bent-handled, 171–72
  care of, 173
  selection of, 75, 172–73
  specifications for, 170–71
batters
  attributes of, 74–75
  drills for, 82–83
  grip of, 76–77, 116
  pointers for, 80–82
  stance of, 77–78, 80, 116–17
  swing of, 79–80
  See also bunts
batting order, 136

blisters, first aid for, 162
body protector, 122, 158
  for women, 173–75
body weights, 153
breast protectors, 173–74
bruises, first aid for, 162
bunts
  classification of, 86–88
  defense against, 68–72, 128
  defined, 83
  drills for, 89–90
  grip in, 83–84
  pitching strategy and, 117
  placement of, 86
  pointers for, 88–89
  stance in, 84–86

catcher
  as backup, 56, 130–31
  drills for, 133–34
  equipment of, 122, 158, 167,
    173–77
  fielding by, 69, 127–28
  responsibilities of, 121–22, 132–
    33
  semicrouch position of, 122–25
  signal calling by, 131–32, 139
  starting position of, 30
  in tag plays, 129–30
  target placement by, 125
  throwing techniques of, 126–27
catching technique
  for bunted ball, 71
  drills on, 17–18
  flight of ball and, 24
  glove in, 13
  lining up with ball, 14–15
  on nonglove side, 16
  one-handed, 15–16
  priority calls in, 48
  running and, 24–25, 47
  weather and, 25
  See also fielding
Catholic Youth Organization of
  the Diocese of Rockville
  Center, softball rules of, 194–
  95, 201–204
center fielder
  backup by, 56
  skills of, 45

change-up pitch, 115–16
coach
  preseason responsibility of,
    184–85
  tryout arrangements by, 185–87
Coaching: Women's Athletics
  (magazine), 196
conditioning. *See* training and
  conditioning
contusions, first aid for, 162
curve ball, 114
cut-off plays, 62–65

dislocations, first aid for, 162
double play
  catcher in, 129
  drills for, 52–54
  forms of, 51–52
  at second base, 34–35
drag bunt, 87
drop ball, 114–15

equipment
  of catcher, 122, 167, 173–77
  injury prevention and, 158
  miscellaneous, 182–83
  selection criteria for, 164–66
  See also specific types
exercises
  on improvised machines, 144–45
  against resistance, 143–44
  softball techniques in, 154–56
  strengthening, 151–54
  stretching, 147–51
  in warm-up period, 145–47
eyeglasses
  catcher's mask with, 175–76
  strap for, 158

field
  reservation of, 192
  safety inspection of, 158–59, 193
fielding
  by catcher, 69, 127–28
  of fly balls, 23–26, 45–46, 47
  of ground balls, 19–23, 47–48
  starting positions in, 28, 29
  See also catching techniques;
    outfielder; throwing
    techniques

first aid
  for common injuries, 162–63
  kits, 160–61
First Aider, The (magazine), 196–97
first-and-third situation, defense in, 72–73
first baseman
  cut-off by, 62–63
  in fielding bunts, 68–69
  footwork of, 31–32
  responsibilities of, 28
  skills of, 30
  starting position of, 28, 30–31
  tag plays by, 33–34
fly balls, fielding of, 23–26, 45–46, 47
footwork
  of first baseman, 31–32
  for throwing, 9, 20
force play, 50–51
fractures, first aid for, 163

game balls, 193
glove(s)
  break-in of, 169–70
  care of, 170
  of catcher, 166–67
  catching technique and, 13, 14–15, 25
  of fielder, 167–68
  multicolor, 168
  selection of, 158, 168–69
glove hand
  for right- and left-handed players, 13, 30
  starting position and, 28
grip
  in batting, 76–77
  for bunts, 83–84
  in pitching, 106–7, 114, 115, 116
  for throwing, 8–9, 14
groin, stretching exercises for, 149
ground ball
  drop pitch for, 114–15
  fielding of, 19–23, 47–48

hand signals
  for base run, 92
  in bunt situations, 68

hand weights, 154
helmet, catcher, 176
hips, stretching exercises for, 147–49
hit, sound of, 24
home plate, 182
home team, responsibilities of, 192–93

infielder
  back-up responsibility of, 56–57
  body position of, 19
  position play by, 27–30
  in relay plays, 58
injury(s)
  common, 157
  first aid for, 160–63, 196–97
  reconditioning after, 159–60
injury prevention
  equipment selection for, 158
  field safety inspection for, 158–59, 193
  muscle flexibility and, 157–58
  during practice and warm-up, 159
  skills instruction and, 159
intentional walk, as pitching strategy, 117
International Federation of Softball, goals of, 2

knee guards, 122

lacerations, first aid for, 163
leagues
  function of, 194
  rules of, 194–95, 201–4
left fielder
  backup by, 54–55
  skills of, 45
left-handed player
  at first base, 30
  glove hand in, 13
leg(s)
  guards, 176–77
  strengthening exercises for, 153
  stretching exercises for, 147–49
lineup, development of, 136

mask, catcher's, 122, 158, 175–76
mitt, 166–67
muscle injuries, prevention of, 157–58

National Association for Girls and Women in Sport (NAGWS), 196
National Collegiate Athletic Association (NCAA), 195
National Junior Collegiate Athletic Association (NJCAA), 195
National Softball Week, 2

Official Guide and Rule Book, 196
opposition, knowledge of, 137
outfielder
  backup by, 54–56
  body position of, 23
  in bunt defense, 71
  drills for, 49–50
  fielding techniques of, 23–26, 45–48
  in relay plays, 59–60
  skills of, 45
overhand throw, 7, 10–11, 46
  glove in, 13
  strengthening exercises for, 153

pitchers and pitching
  attributes of, 104–5
  as backup, 56, 57
  in bunt defense, 69, 70
  drills for, 119–20
  grip of, 106–7, 114, 115, 116
  presentation of ball by, 105–6
  release point of, 75
  responsibilities of, 118–19
  speed *vs.* control in, 118
  spin in, 114–16
  starting position of, 29–30
  strategy of, 116–17
  styles of, 107–13
position play concept, 27
practice sessions, 190–91
  indoor, 191–92
  safety precautions in, 159

preseason period
  organization in, 184–85
  training in, 142–43

Raybestos Breakettes (Stratford, Conn.), 2
relay plays, 57–62
right fielder
  backup by, 55
  skills of, 45
right-handed player, glove hand of, 13
rise ball, 115
rundown play, 65–67
run-and-hit plays, 81
running techniques
  diagonal pattern in, 24–25
  for fly ball catch, 47
  on toes, 24
  See also base running

safety squeeze play, 88
scorebook, 182, 193
second baseman
  as backup, 56
  in bunt defense, 69
  double plays by, 34–35
  responsibilities of, 28
  starting position of, 28–29
  tag plays by, 35–38
shin guards, 122, 158
shoes
  care of, 179
  selection of, 177–79
shortstop
  as backup, 56–57
  in bunt defense, 69–70
  second baseman and, 34–35
  starting position of, 29
shoulder, stretching exercise for, 149–51
sidearm throw, 7–8, 11
  glove in, 13
signals
  from catcher, 131–32, 139
  hand, 68, 92
  team effort and, 138–39
sit-ups, 151–52
skin scrapes, first aid for, 162
slap bunt, 87

slide
  decision making for, 96–97
  head first, 99–100
  hook, 99
  straight-in, 97
slingshot motion, in pitching,
  107–9
slow pitch softball, 2
softball
  benefits of, 4–5
  international growth of, 1–2
  leagues, 194–95
  organizations for, 195–96
  publications on, 196–97
  See also specific subjects
sports, sex discrimination in, 3, 4
sprains, first aid for, 163
square-off stance, 84–85
squeeze bunt, 87–88
starting position, 28–30
stealing bases, batter's role in, 81–
  82
strains, first aid for, 163
strengthening exercises, 151–54
stretching exercises, 147–51
suicide squeeze play, 88

tag plays
  catcher in, 129–30
  foot-body position in, 33–34,
    35–37, 39
  on upright baserunners, 37–38,
    39–40
team concept
  backup role in, 136–37
  communication system in, 138–
    39
  knowledge of opposition in,
    137
  offense–defense relations in,
    139–41
  skill utilization and, 135–36

third baseman
  fielding by, 39–40, 68–69
  responsibilities of, 28
  skills of, 38
  starting position of, 28, 38–39
  taking lead from, 95
throwing techniques, 7–8
  arm motions in, 10–13, 20
  bounce point in, 46
  from catching position, 126–27
  cut-off play and, 62–65
  drills on, 17–18
  footwork in, 9, 20
  grip in, 8–9
  overhand, 46
  relay system in, 57–62
  in rundown play, 65–66
  trajectory in, 46
  See also fielding; pitchers and
    pitching
tournaments, 1, 185, 195–96
training and conditioning, 142–43
  injury reduction and, 157–58
  See also exercises
tryout programs, 185–89

umpires
  arrangements for, 192–93
  fees of, 185
underhand throw, 153
uniforms, 181–82, 185
Universal Gym equipment, 143–44

walk, intentional, 117
warm-up period, 132
  exercises in, 145–47
  in practice, 190
  safety precautions in, 159
women athletes
  myths about, 3–4
  sex discrimination against, 3, 4
wounds, first aid for, 163